KU-352-952

CITYPACK GUIDE TO
Madrid

How to Use This Book

KEY TO SYMBOLS

➕ Map reference to the accompanying fold-out map

✉ Address

☎ Telephone number

🕒 Opening/closing times

🍴 Restaurant or café

🚆 Nearest rail station

Ⓜ Nearest subway (Metro) station

🚌 Nearest bus route

🛥 Nearest riverboat or ferry stop

♿ Facilities for visitors with disabilities

❓ Other practical information

▷ Further information

ℹ Tourist information

✋ Admission charges: Expensive (over €8), Moderate (€5–€8) and Inexpensive (under €5)

This guide is divided into four sections

● Essential Madrid: An introduction to the city and tips on making the most of your stay.

● Madrid by Area: We've broken the city into five areas, and recommended the best sights, shops, entertainment venues, nightlife and places to eat in each one. Suggested walks help you to explore on foot.

● Where to Stay: The best hotels, whether you're looking for luxury, budget or something in between.

● Need to Know: The info you need to make your trip run smoothly, including getting about by public transportation, weather tips, emergency phone numbers and useful websites.

Navigation In the Madrid by Area chapter, we've given each area its own color, which is also used on the locator maps throughout the book and the map on the inside front cover.

Maps The fold-out map with this book is a comprehensive street plan of Madrid. The grid on this fold-out map is the same as the grid on the locator maps within the book. We've given grid references within the book for each sight and listing.

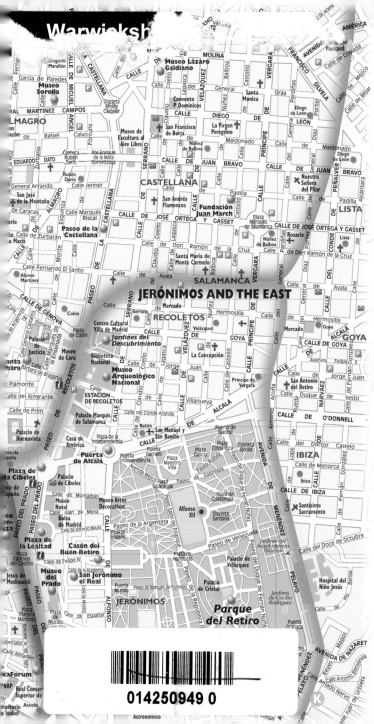

Contents

CONTENTS

Introducing Madrid

Madrid is truly dynamic, successfully combining big-city sophistication with the social conviviality of a small town. One of Europe's liveliest late-night capitals, it also offers stunning architecture, superb museums and fascinating historic sights.

Madrid dates from 1561, when King Felipe II made the city the capital of what soon became the world's biggest empire. Yet nowhere else in the world is the past so close to the present. Nuns and monks still live and worship in convents and monasteries that date back for centuries. Shops still bake traditional cakes and breads; locals stop for olives and a small glass of wine like their forebears have done for generations. But Madrid is also a city known for its exciting modern architecture, for its chic small hotels, for its nightlife, with bars and clubs open till dawn…and beyond. The city is also at the epicenter of the country's fashion industry, with countless Spanish designers as well as the most prestigious international labels represented.

As well as the three internationally acclaimed art museums, Madrid has dozens of smaller galleries and exhibition spaces, covering everything from archaeology to science, which help provide an insight into the glory and grandeur that was imperial Spain. And the city is all so walkable. Stroll around or, if your feet complain, use one of the cleanest, safest and cheapest public transportation systems in the world. It is easy to get anywhere in minutes.

This is a city where you need to go with the flow. Only a foreigner eats dinner as early as 9 at night here; only a foreigner walks the boiling sidewalks on a baking hot afternoon in high summer; only a foreigner spends a whole evening at the same tapas bar. So do as locals do: try different tapas at different bars, head out into the city for dinner at 10pm, take an afternoon nap, then stay up to the small hours.

FACTS AND FIGURES

- The population of Madrid is 3.2 million.
- Madrid is Europe's third-largest city, after London and Berlin.
- Madrid is the highest capital in Europe (646m/2,120ft) and is known for its dry climate, especially in summer.
- Madrid is 300km (190 miles) from the sea.

SIMPLY THE BEST

FIFA, football's governing body, recognized Real Madrid as the world's best football club of the 20th century. You can tour their stadium, named for their former president, Santiago Bernabéu. He was part of a commission set up to promote a new competition—the European Cup. Real Madrid won the first ever European Cup on 13 June 1956.

GOLDEN TRIANGLE

Art buff or not, there is something particularly enthralling about having three of the the country's most prestigious art museums within a short stroll of each other. Be awed by the dark, tumultuous paintings of Goya at Museo del Prado; Picasso's iconic *Guernica* at the Museo Nacional Reina Sofia; and the sheer breadth of styles at the Museum Thyssen-Bornemisza.

MOVIE MAGIC

Acclaimed Spanish cinema director Pedro Almodóvar evidently derives great inspiration from his home city. Many of his films, including *Broken Embraces* (2009) and the more recent *Beautiful Youth* (2014) use Madrid as a backdrop. One of his first films, *Labyrinth of Passion* (1982), was partly shot in the Rastro street market, where Almodóvar once had a stand.

A Short Stay in Madrid

DAY 1

Morning To beat the crowds in the city's three great museums, you need a prompt start. For the **Museo Nacional Reina Sofía** (▷ 46), use the new extension entrance to the museum (off the Glorieta de Carlos V), still undiscovered by the main rush. Go straight up to see Picasso's *Guernica*, then work your way down.

Lunch When the museum gets busy, take the Metro across to Serrano for a smart lunch at **Álbora** (▷ 81) or any of the myriad cafés.

Afternoon Now hit the shops. Work your way up Serrano to the **ABC Serrano Shopping Center** (▷ 94), a gallery of smart boutiques. Stroll down the streets called Goya, Velázquez and Ortega y Gasset. Then go back to your hotel for a siesta.

Evening Linger over tapas in the bars on and around the Plaza de Santa Ana. As well as traditional haunts, such as the Cervecería Alemana, there are contemporary wine bars, such as **La Vinoteca Barbechera** (▷ 66). Stroll down to the **Museo Thyssen-Bornemisza** (▷ 48) and soak up some culture. In July and August, the museum stays open late during *Noches de verano*, Summer Nights.

Dinner Afterward, still in the Museo Thyssen-Bornemisza, dine at the **El Mirador del Museo restaurant**, on the terrace, high above the city.

Later The Spanish love to stay up late, late, late. Hit a popular club such as the **Café Central** (▷ 63) for jazz or the **Casa Patas** (▷ 63) for flamenco. And if you are still going strong at 4am, join the locals at **Chocolatería San Ginés** (▷ 65) for hot chocolate before heading back to your hotel for bed.

DAY 2

Morning If it is a Sunday morning, then do what everyone does: go to El Rastro (▷ 54). This swirling mix of outdoor markets and shops has everything from cheap toys, pottery and clothing to expensive antiques and leather goods. Make sure that you have no tempting cell phone or wallet on view. Afterward, drift through the narrow lanes toward the **Plaza de Tirso de Molina**, with its cheerful flower stands, shiny paving, fountains and statue of Tirso de Molina himself. The real name of this playwright was Gabriel Tellez, and he is best remembered for his character, Don Juan. Stroll on east through the old city streets and join locals grazing along Calle de Jésus at tapas bars such as **Cervecería Cervantes** (▷ 65).

Lunch Instead of a big meal, continue hopping in and out of the line of tapas bars along the street.

Afternoon Cross the Paseo del Prado and watch *madrileños* at play in **Parque del Retiro** (▷ 75). There are puppet shows for little children; boats for hire on the lake; and live concerts in summer, when most people are happy to stretch out on the lawns and snooze.

Evening Another authentic Madrid experience is the *zarzuela.* Part Gilbert and Sullivan, part Feydeau farce, these are Spanish comic operas. The music is jolly, the plots are silly, so you don't need to understand the language. The **Teatro de la Zarzuela** (▷ 64) also stages ballet and dance.

Dinner To keep the Spanish experience going to the end of your day, dine nearby at **Taberna Maceira** (▷ 66), where crowds of locals and visitors alike pack in elbow-to-elbow at wooden tables for hearty and traditional Galician dishes.

▶▶▶

Casa de Campo ▷ 24
Take a break from the artworks in Madrid's vast "green lung".

Catedral de la Almudena ▷ 25 Madrid's most important church has an impressive clifftop setting.

Ermita de San Antonio de la Florida ▷ 26 Superb Goya frescoes in the chapel where he is buried.

Real Madrid ▷ 100
Spain's most illustrious football club has its home at the impressive Santiago Bernabéu stadium.

Real Academia de Bellas Artes ▷ 55 The Fine Arts Academy is best known for its Goya self-portraits.

El Rastro ▷ 54 For bargains galore, the legendary Sunday market still attracts locals and visitors alike.

Puerta del Sol ▷ 53 The 'gateway of the sun' has been the heart of the city since the 15th century.

Plaza de la Paja ▷ 52
Pleasantly peaceful with the remains of the old Bishop's Palace and many outdoor bars and cafés.

Plaza de Oriente ▷ 35
Elegant, pedestrianized square that is a welcome haven of peace in the city.

Plaza Mayor ▷ 51
Madrid's most handsome square, famous for its frescoed Casa de la Panedería.

Plaza de la Cibeles ▷ 76–77 The Cibeles Fountain is the city's best-loved landmark.

Parque del Retiro ▷ 74–75 Enjoy the shady paths and formal gardens of Madrid's central park.

These pages are a quick guide to the Top 25, which are described in more detail later. Here they are listed alphabetically, and the tinted background shows which area they are in.

Map areas:

Real Madrid

CHUECA AND THE NORTH 81–94

EL VISO
RÍOS ROSAS
Parque Santa Engracia
CHAMBERÍ
Museo Sorolla
Museo Lázaro Galdiano
RAFALGAR
ALMAGRO
CASTELLANA
LISTA
SALAMANCA
RECOLETOS
JUSTICIA
Jardines del Descubrimiento
JERÓNIMOS AND THE EAST 67–80
GOYA
Museo Arqueológico Nacional
Monasterio de las Descalzas Reales
SOL
Plaza de la Cibeles
IBIZA
Real Academia de Bellas Artes
Puerta del Sol
CORTES
Museo Thyssen-Bornemisza
Jardines del Arquit Herrero Palacios
RETIRO
CENTRO
Museo del Prado
JERÓNIMOS
Jardines de Cecilio Rodríguez
NIÑO JESÚS
CENTRO 43–66
Real Jardín Botánico
Parque del Retiro
La Rosaleda
Museo Nacional Reina Sofía
Viveros Municipales
EMBAJADORES
PACÍFICO

Shopping

The range of shopping available in Madrid is wonderfully diverse. Small idiosyncratic shops that have been in the same family for generations have managed to survive despite the influx of national and global chains and the increase in out-of-town malls. Most *barrios* (neighborhoods) also have a bustling *mercado* (indoor food market), selling everything from bunches of fragrant herbs to fresh olives and artisanal bread. For the quintessential *madrileño* shopping experience, however, head to the fascinating Sunday Rastro flea market.

A Bit of Everything

It's not just what shops sell that is so eclectic—how they look is also diverse. Temples of consumerism in steel and glass happily rub shoulders with cramped, dark shops where the stock is piled high and the merchandise is highly specialized. Few other world capitals have as many stores devoted to so many oddities—outsize corsetry, plaster statuary, crystallized violets. This gives Madrid shopping a special appeal, whether you're after easy-to-carry souvenirs or seriously self-indulgent retail therapy, or you simply enjoy window-shopping.

Clothes and Accessories

Madrid has branches of some of Europe and Spain's best-known fashion stores, as well as

WHERE TO SHOP

Ask a *madrileño* where to find the city's shopping heart and the answer is bound to be around Calle Preciados, the pedestrianized street that connects Puerta del Sol with the Gran Vía. Here you'll find branches of all the big chain stores, as well as Madrid's biggest department store, and everything from fashion to food. Smarter by far are the quiet, well-heeled streets of the Salamanca district, home to the big designer names and luxury stores of all description. The best places to trawl for souvenirs are around Plaza Mayor or Malasaña. Head to Chueca for cutting-edge style and street fashion.

Clockwise from top left: Flamenco shop; stallholders at El Rastro flea market spread their wares out on the ground; lace-edged

the latest in the stylish chain-store fashion, like Zara, for which Spain is renowned. Spanish leather shoes, bags and belts are some of the best in Europe, and excellent value.

Gifts

For gifts, you'll find goods from all over Spain, ranging from the tasteful fringed and embroidered shawls and lacy mantillas (traditionally worn over a high comb), warm winter capes, elegant hats, delicate china, traditional ceramics and damascene work, to the marvelously tacky (plastic flamenco dolls, a poster of a *torero* with your name on it, and metal Don Quixotes).

Food

Comestibles makes a great souvenir or gift. In addition to the obvious olive oil, nougat or chocolate, hunt down saffron, and the wonderful dried nuts, seeds and fruits so loved by the Spanish. Or look for convent-baked biscuits or cakes, vacuum-packed *jamón* (dry-cured ham), *chorizo* (spicy sausage) or *morcilla* (unctuous black pudding).

Tax Refunds and Sales

IVA (sales tax) is added at 10 percent on food and 21 percent on most other items. Non-EU visitors can reclaim the IVA on purchases, but the total must be at least €90.16, paid in a single store in a single day. Stores taking part display a Tax-Free shopping sticker. For more detailed information, see globalblue.com. Sales generally run from mid-January to February, and July to August.

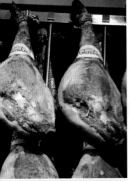

fans; shop window in Calle de Serrano; legs of ham; stall at the Rastro; designer fashion store in the upmarket Salamanca district

---

MARKETS

Markets are not only a window into everyday life, but also the perfect place to pick up a picnic to eat in the park. Some of the best are La Cebada (🚇 La Latina)—for a huge range of goods and low prices; El Rastro (▷ 54, 🚇 Tirso de Molina)—the famous Sunday market; and La Paz (🚇 Serrano)—for quality and varied produce aimed at the prosperous Salamanca inhabitants.

Shopping by Theme

Whether you're looking for a department store, a quirky boutique, or something in between, you'll find it all in Madrid. On this page shops are listed by theme. For a more detailed write-up, see the individual listings in Madrid by Area.

Antiques and Gifts
Felix Antigüedades (▷ 61)
Galerías Piquér (▷ 62)
Museo del Prado (▷ 80)
Museo del Traje (▷ 39)

Fashion/Accessories
Fansi (▷ 39)
Massimo Dutti Woman (▷ 39)
Piel de Toro (▷ 80)
Purificación García (▷ 94)

Food and Wine
Antigua Pastelería del Pozo (▷ 61)
Cacao Sampaka (▷ 94)
Maria Cabello (▷ 62)
Mariano Madrueño (▷ 62)
Reserva y Cata (▷ 94)
Tienda Olivarero (▷ 94)

Shoes/Accessories
Guantes Luque (▷ 62)
Ioli (▷ 94)
Tino González (▷ 39)
La Violeta (▷ 62)

Shopping Malls and Department Stores
ABC Serrano Shopping Center (▷ 94)
Centro Comercial Príncipe Pío (▷ 39)
El Corte Inglés (▷ 61)
FNAC (▷ 61)
El Jardín de Serrano (▷ 80)

Something Different
Berbería del Sahara y El Sahel (▷ 39)
Cuesta Moyano (▷ 80)
El Flamenco Vive (▷ 61)
Hoss (▷ 94)
Imaginarium (▷ 80)

Lfont Tea Mountain (▷ 39)
Natura (▷ 80)
Objetos de Arte Toledano (▷ 80)
Perfumería Alvarez Gomez (▷ 80)

Traditional
Amparo Mercería (▷ 61)
Antigua Casa Talavera (▷ 61)
Casa de Diego (▷ 61)
La Favorita (▷ 61)
Gil (▷ 62)
Guitarras Ramírez (▷ 62)
Seseña (▷ 62)

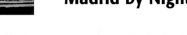

Madrid by Night

Madrid has a year-round agenda of cultural events, from opera, orchestral concerts, plays, dance and original-language films to jazz, flamenco and Latin American music.

A Quiet Evening

With little hope of a restaurant dinner before 9, you might want to take your evening stroll before you eat. Touristy though it is, the Plaza Mayor looks great by night; from here you can wander through buzzing Huertas down to the Paseo del Prado, a wonderful place in summer for a drink at a *terraza*. A few minutes' walk away lies Retiro Park, perfect on balmy evenings. For window shopping, head for the elegant streets of Salamanca or lively Chueca.

Night Owls

Madrid's reputation as an all-night party town is deserved. Nightlife concentrates around Huertas, Lavapiés, Malasaña and off Sol. Gay-oriented Chueca is fashionably cool and Salamanca is for a dressed-up occasion. But be warned: don't go out too early or you might think there is no action. A night out in Madrid can start at 10 or 11pm or even later, particularly on weekends and in the summer.

Details

Get information in the weekly entertainment guide *Guía del Ocio* (guiadelocio.com) and reserve tickets for concerts and plays via entradas.com.

From top: Flamenco show; flamenco musicians performing; flamenco dancer; traditional taberna *sign*

FLOODLIT STONE

Great cities look wonderful under floodlights and Madrid is no exception. Imaginative lighting enhances much of the city after dark. Don't miss the subtly lit charms of the Plaza Mayor, then enjoy the brilliance lighting adds to the Palacio Real and the Plaza de Oriente. The Paseo del Prado is beautifully illuminated at night; admire the sparkle of light on the water of the fountains in Plaza de la Cibeles and Plaza de Canovas de Castillo before stopping at one of the summertime *terrazas*.

Where to Eat

Madrid is increasingly becoming a foodie capital. You can enjoy regional food from all over the peninsula here, as well as superb tapas, snacks and dishes from farther afield and innovative contemporary cuisine.

Where to Eat

There's a huge choice of eating places in Madrid, particularly around Sol, Santa Ana and Huertas, and the Latina, Lavapiés, Chueca and Malasaña districts. The city's smartest and priciest restaurants are concentrated near the Paseo del Prado and the Retiro and scattered throughout Salamanca. The IVA tax of 10 percent is added to bills in restaurants and bars. As for tipping, it is customary to leave a few coins in a bar and 5 percent in a restaurant.

Types of Restaurant

Restaurantes are officially graded with one to five forks, and range from simple establishments serving up the trusty *menú del día* to very grand—and pricey—venues. Tapas bars are quintessentially Spanish. These snacks range from a few olives or almonds to wedges of tortilla, shellfish, meat croquettes and wonderful vegetable dishes laced with garlic. All tapas bars have their own special dishes, and locals move from place to place, ordering the dishes that each bar does particularly well. The barman normally keeps track of what you've had and you pay at the end. The city has a very active café life, with wonderful old places where you can read the papers and watch the world go by.

MEAL TIMES

The Spanish usually eat breakfast (*desayuno*) between 9 and 10, though it is served earlier in hotels. It's usually sweet—*chocolate con churros* (hot chocolate and stick-shaped doughnuts) or toast with jam. Traditionally, the main meal of the day, lunch (*almuerzo*) is from 2 to 4. The Spanish eat dinner (*cena*) any time after 9.30 through till midnight. But, with cafés and tapas bars open long hours, you can always find something tasty to eat.

From top: Tapas bar; pinchos (snacks skewered with a cocktail stick); taberna sign; tapas dishes

Where to Eat by Cuisine

There are plenty of places to eat to suit all tastes and budgets in Madrid. On this page they are listed by cuisine. For a more detailed description of each restaurant, see Madrid by Area.

Basque and Catalan
Dantxari (▷ 41)
Taberna del Alabardero (▷ 42)

Cafés
Café Manuela (▷ 95)
Café de Ruiz (▷ 95)
Chocolatería San Ginés (▷ 65)

Galician and Asturian
Casa Mingo (▷ 41)
El Escarpín (▷ 42)
La Hoja (▷ 82)
Taberna Maceira (▷ 66)

Contemporary Cuisine
Álbora (▷ 81)
Club Allard (▷ 41)
DSTAgE (▷ 96)
La Gamella (▷ 82)
Mercado de San Miguel (▷ 66)
Restaurante Viridiana (▷ 82)

Italian
Trattoria Sant'Arcangelo (▷ 82)

Mexican
Entre Suspiro y Suspiro (▷ 41)

Spanish
El Bierzo (▷ 96)
El Botánico (▷ 81)
El Ingenio (▷ 42)
Mercado de San Antón (▷ 96)
La Montería (▷ 82)
Posada de la Villa (▷ 65)
Prada a Tope (▷ 42)
La Sacristía (▷ 96)
Sal Gorda (▷ 42)
El Senador (▷ 42)
Viuda de Vacas (▷ 66)

Tapas
Baztán (▷ 96)
Los Caracoles (▷ 65)

Casa Alberto (▷ 65)
Casa Labra (▷ 65)
Casa Revuelta (▷ 65)
Cervecería Cervantes (▷ 65)
Lhardy (▷ 65)
Sanlúcar (▷ 42)
Taberna de Antonio Sánchez (▷ 66)
La Vinoteca Barbechera (▷ 66)

Traditional Madrid Cuisine
La Bola (▷ 41)
Botín (▷ 65)
Café de Oriente (▷ 41)
La Castela (▷ 82)
Posada de la Villa (▷ 66)

Top Tips For...

These great suggestions will help you tailor
your ideal visit to Madrid, no matter how
you choose to spend your time. Each entry
has a fuller write-up elsewhere in the book.

PEOPLE-WATCHING
Grab a table at the Café de Oriente terrace
overlooking a pretty plaza with the Royal Palace
beyond (▷ 41).
Stroll around Plaza Mayor, the city's
emblematic main square, famed for its
sumptuous architecture and flanked by
sidewalk cafés (▷ 51).
Take a ride in a rowing boat on the lake in
Retiro park (▷ 75).
Ride the *teleférico* (cable car) for a bird's-eye
view of the city (▷ 34).

SHOPPING TILL YOU DROP
Check out ABC Serrano—a small and classy
mall in the heart of an up-market shopping
area (▷ 94).
Head to El Rastro on a Sunday morning to
browse the fun flea market (▷ 54).
El Corte Inglés is Spain's top department store
(▷ 61).
Go antiques shopping in Galerías Piquér mall
in the Rastro street (▷ 62).

CHECKING OUT GREAT ART
The Prado is the city's most famous museum,
displaying a vast wealth of art (▷ 72).
See Picasso's *Guernica*, and a vast collection
of contemporary art, at Museo Nacional Reina
Sofía (▷ 47).
Museo Thyssen-Bornemisza specializes in
19th-century American art (▷ 48).

SPLASHING OUT
For top-quality ceramics, check out Antigua
Casa Talavera (▷ 61).
For exquisite fans, most of them hand-pianted,
try Casa de Diego (▷ 61).
Seseña offers classic Spanish capes (▷ 62).

*Clockwise from top
left: the teleférico; the
Bernabéu stadium;
flamingos in the Casa*

GREEN SPACES

Vast El Retiro park is great for picnics and leisurely strolls (▷ 75).

Real Jardín Botanico is a tranquil oasis in the heart of the city (▷ 79).

Parque del Oeste is a delightful park with ornamental statues, a rose garden and a genuine Egyptian temple (▷ 34).

For wonderful city views, find the small Jardines de Las Vistillas (▷ 37).

See the superb sculptures in the Jardines del Descubrimiento (▷ 78).

Casa de Campo is known as the lungs of the city, thanks to its great size (▷ 24).

KEEPING KIDS HAPPY

Take a horse-drawn carriage ride in Retiro park (▷ 75).

Get the adrenaline pumping on the rides in Parque de Atracciones amusement park in Casa de Campo (▷ 24).

Dress up in 18th-century garb at the Museo del Traje (▷ 31).

Run around the play areas in renovated Plaza de Santa Ana (▷ 59) or the new riverside park Madrid Río (▷ 101).

KEEPING TO A TIGHT BUDGET

Check out the free concerts in the Retiro park (▷ 75).

Trace Madrid's fascinating history at the superb Museo de Historia de Madrid, which has free entry (▷ 90).

Museo Nacional Reina Sofia is free to visit on Saturday afternoons and Sunday (▷ 46).

TRADITIONAL TAPAS

Baztán is a charming traditional taberna with a sprawling terrace (▷ 96).

Taberna de Antonio Sánchez is an intimate and relaxed small bar (▷ 66).

To sample snails, seek out Los Caracoles (▷ 65).

Enjoy traditional Andalucian tapas in charming Sanlúcar (▷ 42).

de Campo zoo; tapas; dazzling fans; Palacio de Cristal in the Retiro park

OLD-FASHIONED FEASTING

The world's oldest restaurant is in Madrid—Botín (▷ 65).

Sample Galician cooking, especially *pulpo* (octopus) at Taberna Maceira (▷ 66).

Posada de la Villa specializes in traditional Madrid oven-roast lamb (▷ 66).

Taberna del Alabardero has views of the palace and a sophisticated menu (▷ 42).

La Bola has been run by the same family since 1870; come here to sample a traditional Madrid stew (▷ 41).

FASHIONABLE HOTELS

Hospes Puerto de Alcalá is a new boutique hotel in a classic building (▷ 112).

ME Madrid is an elegant and comfortable hotel right on one of Madrid's most attractive squares (▷ 112).

Hotel Puerta América is a standout hotel for its contemporary avant-garde decor and superb location (▷ 112).

Quo is a small chain of fashionable hotels in the city (▷ 112).

CELEB-SPOTTING

Bar Skynight, on top of Hotel Puerta América (Avenida de América) has stunning views (▷ 112).

Fortuny attracts elegant clubbers with its eclectic mix of music (▷ 95).

Glass Bar, at the sophisticated Hotel Urban, is famous for its transparent chairs (▷ 64).

PARTYING TILL DAWN

For that beach party vibe, the indoor beach at Ojalá is a must (▷ 95).

Live DJs and jam sessions keep Marula Café buzzing all night (▷ 40).

Seven dance floors offering everything from house to Latin make Teatro Kapital one of the city's most famous venues to party (▷ 81).

Enormous and fun, Joy Eslava has been a staple on the Madrid club scene for decades (▷ 64).

From top: Restaurante Botín; fashionable hotels abound; cocktails; clubbing

Madrid by Area

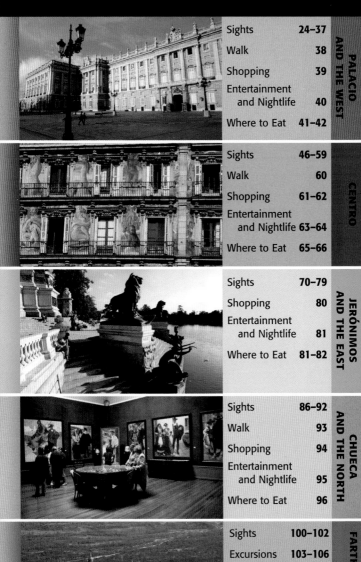

The Royal Palace is now a museum, but this area retains the elegance of the past. There are also plenty of green spaces.

Palacio and the West

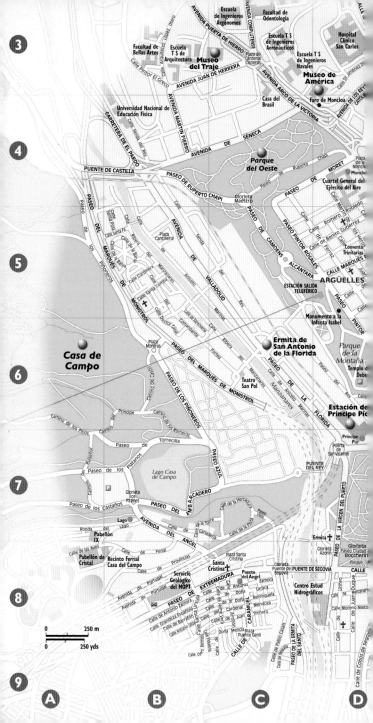

Casa de Campo

TOP 25

Flamingos in the zoo (left); running in Casa de Campo (right)

THE BASICS

🚌 A6

✉ Calle Marqués de Monistrol, Avenida de Portugal

🚇 Lago, Batán, Casa de Campo

🚌 25, 33, 65

Parque de Atracciones

parquedeatracciones.es

🚌 A6

🕐 Jun to mid-Sep daily noon–dusk; mid-Sep to Mar Sat–Sun noon–dusk; Easter week daily noon–dusk; Apr Fri–Sun noon–dusk; May Tue–Sun noon–dusk

🍴 Cafés, restaurants

🚇 Batán

🚌 33, 65

♿ Good

💰 Expensive

Zoo-Aquarium de Madrid

zoomadrid.com

🚌 A6

🕐 Mon–Fri 11–dusk, Sat–Sun 10.30–dusk

🍴 Cafés, restaurants

🚇 Batán, Casa de Campo

🚌 33

♿ Good

💰 Expensive

TIP

● This huge park is ideal for cycling, and several companies offer bike tours, including Bim Bim Bikes (bimbim.com)

That Madrid is one of Europe's greenest capitals is mainly because of the 1,722ha (4,255-acre) Casa de Campo, stretching away to the northwest. Once a royal hunting estate, it was opened to the public in 1931, quickly becoming popular as a cool haven in Madrid's hot summer.

Wide open space In Casa de Campo, you can walk for a couple of hours without being interrupted (though this is best avoided after dark). During the Civil War, Franco's troops were based here, and signs of trenches are still visible. The park contains sports facilities, including an open-air pool, a large lake (where you can hire boats), amusement park, aquarium and zoo. The *teleférico* (cable car, teleferico.com) runs up here from the Parque del Oeste (▷ 34), and the 11-minute journey is an excellent way to arrive, affording superb views over the city.

Parque de Atracciones This amusement park has more than 40 rides, from gentle merry-go-rounds to the breathtaking Abismo rollercoaster and the 63m (207ft) sheer vertical drop of La Lanzadera. There are open-air concerts in summer.

The zoo Madrid's zoo is one of the best in Europe. It contains more than 2,000 animals and more than 100 species of bird. There is a dolphinarium, a train ride, an aquarium and a children's section. Parrot shows, the shark tank and birds of prey are all popular.

Inside (left) the neo-classical Catedral de la Almudena (middle and right)

TOP
25

Catedral de la Almudena

PALACIO AND THE WEST TOP 25

Madrid's cathedral took more than 100 years to complete and reflects various architectural schools. Highlights within include a lovely 16th-century altarpiece of the Virgin and beautiful modern stained-glass windows.

A long delay Just 25 years ago, Madrid lacked a cathedral, incredible though it may seem. The first plans for the Almudena, constructed on what was formerly the site of Muslim Madrid's principal mosque, were drawn up in 1879 under Alfonso XII by the architect Giambattista Sacchetti. Redesigned in 1883, it is based on the pattern of a 13th-century cathedral, with a chancel similar to the one at Rheims. A neoclassical style was introduced into the design in 1944, but it wasn't until 1993 that the cathedral was consecrated by the Pope. The main entrance is opposite the Royal Palace; the entrance to the crypt, which houses the Almudena Virgin, is along La Cuesta de la Vega.

The story of the Almudena Virgin According to legend, the image of the Virgin over the entrance had been hidden in the 11th century by Mozarabs. When Spanish hero El Cid reconquered Madrid, he ordered that the image be found, but without success. Alfonso VI then instructed the people of Madrid to dismantle the city walls to find the image. When they reached the grain deposits, they heard a noise from the turrets above, which then collapsed, revealing an image of the Virgin and Child.

THE BASICS

✚ E7

✉ Calle Bailén. Next to Palacio Real

☎ 91 542 22 00

🕐 Daily 9–8.30

Ⓜ Ópera

🚌 3, 31, 148

♿ Good

🎫 Free

HIGHLIGHTS

● Virgin of Almudena
● Coffin of San Isidro
● Dome 20m (66ft) in diameter
● Grenzing organ
● The 104m (340ft)-long nave
● 12 statues of the apostles
● Ornate ceiling

Ermita de San Antonio de la Florida

The facade of the hermitage (left); the exterior (right)

HIGHLIGHTS

● Cupola
● Balustrade
● Marble and stucco font (1798)
● *Lápida de Goya*
● Mirrors under the cupola
● High altar
● Lamp under the cupola (18th-century)
● *San Luis and San Isidro*, Jacinto Gómez Pastor

TIP

● Hours can vary to those stated, especially in July and August.

A national monument, this charming, simple church is the burial site of Goya and home to several of his stunning, recently restored, frescoes.

Resting place Both church and hermitage—the latter to the left as you face the two buildings—are off the beaten track, but worth visiting both for their intimacy and for Goya's frescoes. The original hermitage was begun in 1792 by Charles IV's Italian architect, Francisco Fontana. Goya's remains were buried here in 1919, but without his head: it is said that it was stolen by scientists who wished to study it.

The frescoes Painted using a technique that was revolutionary at the time, the frescoes are distinguished by their richness of color. They tell the life of St. Anthony, representing the saint raising a murdered man from the dead to enable him to name his murderer and spare the life of the innocent accused. The models for the frescoes were members of the Spanish court, but they also included other less reputable figures—by placing rogues alongside the court officials, Goya may have been indicating his contempt for the court of the time.

Girlfriends and boyfriends St. Anthony is the patron saint of sweethearts, and every 13 June girls come here to pray for a boyfriend. Thirteen pins are placed inside the font; when a girl puts her hand in, the number of pins that stick indicates how many beaux she will have that year.

*The Monastery of the
Incarnation (left);
St. Teresa in stained
glass (right)*

TOP 25

Monasterio de la Encarnación

Located away from the traffic of Calle Bailén, the Monastery of the Incarnation is suffused with religious calm that brings peace to the soul.

History Designed by Juan Gómez de Mora in 1611 on instructions from Queen Margarita, wife of Felipe III, the church in the Royal Monastery is typical of Habsburg Spanish religious architecture. Originally the monastery was connected by a passage to the Arab fortress where the Royal Palace now stands. The church was damaged by fire in 1734, and reconstructed in classical-baroque style; the granite facade is all that remains of the original. A 45-minute guided tour leads you through the monastery, which is still used by a community of around 20 Augustinian nuns; it includes the Royal Room, hung with uninspired portraits of the royal family, and the pretty church, which includes a reliquary and musem.

The Reliquary In the middle of the church stand an altar and altarpiece depicting the Holy Family by Bernadino Luini, a pupil of Leonardo da Vinci, and an ornate tabernacle in bronze and rock crystal. Inside is a crucifix of Christ with a crown of thorns, oddly charred: tradition holds that these are the remains of a crucifix defiled by heretics. Among the 1,500 relics on display, in a small glass globe to the right of the entrance, is the dried blood of St. Pantaleón, which is said to mysteriously liquify every year on 27 July, St. Pantaleón's Day.

THE BASICS

patrimonionacional.es
➕ E7
✉ Plaza de la Encarnación 1
☎ 91 454 88 00
🕐 Monastery and Reliquary: Tue–Sat 10–2, 4–6.30, Sun 10–3
Ⓜ Ópera
🚌 25, 39, 148
♿ None
💰 Moderate

HIGHLIGHTS

● *John the Baptist* by Jusepe Ribera
● *Handing over of the Princesses,* anonymous painting in lobby
● *Recumbent Christ* by Gregorio Fernández
● Royal Room
● Altarpiece
● Cupola, with frescoes by González Velázquez
● Frescoes by Francisco Bayeu
● Charred crucifix
● Blood of St. Pantaleón

PALACIO AND THE WEST TOP 25

Museo de Cerralbo

HIGHLIGHTS

- Grand staircase
- *Ecstasy of St. Francis* by El Greco
- *Jacob with his Flock* by José de Ribera
- *Devotion* by Alonso Cano
- *Immaculate Conception* by Francisco Zurbarán
- *Porcupines and Snakes* by Frans Snyders
- Sword collection from the courts of Louis XV and XVI
- Monumental mystery clock

TIP

- The audio guides, in English, are informative.

Idiosyncratic and intermittently splendid, this delightful museum gives you an indication of how the nobility of Madrid lived 100 years ago, in particular the extravagant and fascinating Marquis de Cerralbo.

Home life From the outside, the late 19th-century home of the 17th Marquis of Cerralbo doesn't look particularly splendid. But the clutter of artifacts inside is quite fascinating, and, uniquely among the house-museums in Madrid, the collections are rivaled by the architecture and decor of the rooms themselves, ranging from the frankly shabby to the magnificent. Politician, man of letters and collector, the Marquis donated the house and its contents to the state in 1922, stipulating that his collection be displayed exactly as he had

left it. This is a unique opportunity to see a near-intact aristocrat's home of the turn from the 20th century.

The collection A magnificent grand staircase by Soriano Fort is to your right as you enter. On the second floor, the most notable exhibit is El Greco's striking *Ecstasy of St. Francis* (1600–05) in the chapel. In the gallery surrounding the patio, there are works by Ribera, Van Dyck and Alonso Cano, as well as haunting Alessandro Magnasco landscapes. On the third floor there are collections of weaponry, a dining room containing a remarkable Frans Snyders painting, and an appealingly homey library. Pride of place is given to the sumptuous mirrored ballroom on the first floor, which displays the Marquis's Saxon porcelain, as well as intricate clocks.

THE BASICS

museocerralbo.mcu.es

✛ E6

✉ Calle Ventura Rodríguez 17

☎ 91 547 36 46

🕐 Tue–Sat 9.30–3, Thu 5–8pm, Sun 10–3

🚇 Ventura Rodríguez, Plaza de España

🚌 1, 2, 44, 46, 74, 133, C1, C2

♿ Moderate; call in advance of visit

👜 Inexpensive. Free Sat 2–3, Thu 5–8 and Sun

Museo de América

TOP 25

An equestrian statue set in the form of a tree trunk (right) at the American Museum (left)

THE BASICS

mecd.gob.es/
museodeamerica

🚌 D3

✉ Avenida Reyes Católicos 6

☎ 91 549 26 41

🕐 Tue–Sat 9.30–3, Sun 10–3

🚇 Moncloa, Islas Filipinos

🚌 Circular, 1, 2, 16, 44, 46, 61, 82, 113, 132, 133

♿ Excellent

💶 Inexpensive. Free Sun

HIGHLIGHTS

● Canoe and tipi (Area 6)
● Statues of tribal chieftains (Area 3)
● Painting of *Entrance of Viceroy Morcillo into Potosí* (Area 3)
● Shrunken heads (Area 5)
● Mummy of Parácas (Area 4)
● Treasure of the Quimbayas (Area 4)
● 'Day of the Dead' paraphernalia (Area 4)
● Trocortesiano Maya Codex (Area 5)

This excellent museum in the university district of Moncloa is arranged into themed areas set around a central courtyard. The vast collection covers the archaeological and ethnographical history of the Americas.

History This museum is the best place in Spain to learn about the history of the different races and cultures of the Americas. Gold drew the Spanish to South America and gold draws visitors to marvel at the skills of the pre-Columbian artists. Many artworks were melted down, so what is on show is even more important. With its grand staircase, courtyard and marble floors, the elegant building, dating from 1954, creates the perfect setting for the exhibits.

Layout It's best to follow the suggested route on the map provided. The collection, spread over two floors, divides into five themed areas, including the discovery of the Americas, religion, society and communication. Two particular highlights are the Treasure of the Quimbayas from Colombia, including solid gold figures, and the Trocortesiano Maya Codex (Area 5), which records the Spanish Conquest in minute, intricate runes, and is one of only four pre-Hispanic Mayan codices preserved in the world. The museum has plenty to entertain children as well, including the re-creation of a tipi (Area 6) and (possibly!) the shrunken heads in Area 5, including one of a monkey used as a decorative pendant in a necklace.

One of the men's costumes on display (right) at the Museum of Costume (left)

Museo del Traje

THE BASICS

museodeltraje.mcu.es

➕ C3

✉ Avenida Juan de Herrera 2

☎ 91 550 47 00

🕐 Tue–Sat 9.30–7, Sun 10–3

🍴 Café, restaurant

Ⓜ Moncloa, Ciudad Universitaria

🚌 46, 82, 83, 84, 132, 133

♿ Good

🎟 Inexpensive. Free to under-18s, over-65s; Sat after 2.30pm, Sun

The Museum of Costume explores how Spanish society has changed over the centuries through its fascinating exhibits of clothes and costumes.

The collection In the 14 galleries of this elegant museum, the clothes are shown at different angles, so that you can see the front of some, the back of others. Through the glass, you can peer at centuries-old frock coats and silk doublets, and admire the embroidery on bodices. A fraction of the collection's 21,000 items is on display. The galleries are organized chronologically, showing how fashion evolved over centuries, both in style and practicality. The most delicate pieces cannot be on display for long, so exhibits are routinely changed.

Hi-tech display Historians are fascinated by the 13th-century trousseau of the daughter of Ferdinand III, while many visitors find themselves sidetracked by a hi-tech display devoted to women's underwear. Virtual reality video twirls viewers from the bodices of the 17th century to the girdles of the 1940s. The museum covers everything, from Spanish mantillas to the latest shoes. Whole rooms are dedicated to Spain's legendary fashion designers, such as Mariano Fortuny (born in Granada) and Cristóbal Balenciaga, a Basque who went on to take the Parisian fashion world by storm. Best of all, you can try on some of the clothes to get a feel of how comfortable—or otherwise—they were.

HIGHLIGHTS

● The funerary apparel of Doña María, daughter of Fernando III
● 1740s silver frock coat
● Women's underwear
● Spanish headdresses
● Regional costume
● Fortuny
● Christian Dior
● Pedro Rodríguez and the New Look
● The catwalk

TIPS

● Book up for a special meal at the Café de Oriente (▷ 41), the museum's sophisticated restaurant. In summer, dine out on the terrace.
● Excellent shop, with high-quality silk ties, Spanish shawls and jewelry.

31

Palacio Real

HIGHLIGHTS

● Grand staircase
● Sala de Porcelana
● Salón de Alabarderos
● Salón de Columnas
● Sala de Gasparini
● Salón de Carlos III
● Clock collection
● Chapel by Giambattista Sacchetti and Ventura Rodríguez
● Music Museum
● Sabatini Gardens

TIP

● The Changing of the Guard takes place at noon on the first Wed of the month (not Jul, Aug, Sep).

This magnificent 18th-century royal palace is built entirely of granite and white stone on an awesome scale, and is further enhanced by extensive gardens.

Scaled to fit The Royal Palace was begun under Felipe V in 1737, after the old Muslim fortress was destroyed by fire in 1734. The original design by Filippo Juvanna was for facades measuring 475m (520 yards) each, or three times longer than the palace now, but there was neither the space nor the money for that. It was completed in 1764, to designs by Sacchetti. From the street side, it is a normal palatial building of the period, with Ionic pilasters framing the reception hall windows. The royal family does not actually live here: it is used occasionally for state visits, during which

Clockwise from far left: The facade of the Palacio Real; statues lining the approach; guards outside the palace; a guard taking part in the changing of the guard ceremony; the exterior of the Royal Palace; changing of the guard, involving 100 guards and 100 horses

dinner is served in the gala dining room. The entrance is to the south side of the building, across the Plaza de la Armería, which is flanked by the Royal Armory housing El Cid's sword and the ornate armor of Carlos V and Felipe III.

Interior and gardens There are more than 3,000 rooms, and most are never used. A ceiling by Conrado Giaquinto accents the grand staircase. The stucco ceiling of the Sala de Gasparini is remarkable, while the ceiling of the Sala de Porcelana, built for Carlos III, has a fine display of porcelain plaques. To the north of the palace are the elegant Sabatini Gardens, which offer the best view of the palace, while to the rear is the Campo del Moro. The only way to see the palace is by following a fixed itinerary, which takes in the finest rooms.

THE BASICS

patrimonionacional.es

✚ E7

✉ Calle Bailén

☎ 91 454 88 00

🕐 Apr–Sep daily 10–8, Oct–Mar daily 10–6. Closed during public events

🚇 Ópera

🚌 3, 25, 39, 148

♿ Very good

💰 Expensive. Free to under-5s

Parque del Oeste

The rose garden (left); remains of the Templo de Debod (right)

THE BASICS

➕ C4
✉ Paseo Ruperto Chapi
☎ 91 548 95 12
🎫 Teleférico: check online at teleferico.com
🚇 Moncloa, Príncipe Pío, Plaza de España
🚌 21, 46, 74, 160, 161

Templo de Debod
esmadrid.com
✉ Calle de Ferraz 1, Parque de la Montaña
☎ 91 366 74 15
🎫 Apr–Sep Tue–Fri 10–2, 6–8, Sat–Sun 10–2; Oct–Mar Tue–Fri 9.45–1.45, 4.15–6.15, Sat–Sun 10–2
🚇 Plaza de España, Ventura Rodríguez
🚌 1, 2, 44, 133, 138
🖐 Free

HIGHLIGHTS

● *Teleférico*
● La Rosaleda
● Fuente (fountain)
● Statue of Sor Juana Inés de la Cruz
● Statue of Simón Bolívar
● View over Casa de Campo
● Trees, including Atlas cedar and magnolia

TIP

● Head to the quieter northern end to escape the crowds in summer.

The Parque del Oeste is the best place in the city for a peaceful stroll and more informal than the Retiro. The Montaña del Príncipe Pío, at the park's southern end, is one of the highest points in the city and affords fabulous views.

Rubbish dump to park Designed in the first years of the 20th century on what had previously been an immense rubbish heap, the Parque del Oeste was practically destroyed during the Civil War, when it provided a cover for the Republicans as the Nationalist troops invaded Madrid. It is now one of the city's most appealing and romantic open spaces. The park contains birch, fir, Atlas cedar and cypress trees, among others, as well as a particularly beautiful rose garden, La Rosaleda, which hosts a rose festival each May. The *teleférico* (cable car) in the park runs out to the Casa de Campo, with bird's-eye views over the west of Madrid. In summer, pleasant *terrazas* (terrace bars) are set up along the Paseo de Pintor Rosales, Ernest Hemingway's favorite street.

Templo de Debod One of Madrid's most interesting attractions is not Spanish at all. The Debod Temple, at the park's southern corner, is a fourth-century BC Egyptian temple honoring the god Amon. It was installed in 1970 as a gift from the Egyptian government to Spanish engineers and archaeologists who had saved many treasures before land was flooded after the completion of the Aswan Dam.

Plaza de Oriente

Statues in the Plaza de Oriente, including an equestrian statue of Felipe IV (middle)

Have a drink on the terrace of the neo-baroque Café de Oriente, with the harmonious Jardines Cabo Naval gardens stretching away in front of you to the Royal Palace. This elegant pedestrianized plaza is one of the loveliest squares in the city and the perfect place to people-watch and while away some time.

Ambitious emperor The elegant Plaza de Oriente was planned in 1811 under Joseph Bonaparte. To build it, he had to destroy the monuments and churches that then surrounded the Royal Palace. His original aim had been to build a kind of Champs-Élysées, running from the Plaza to the Cibeles Fountain, but, perhaps fortunately, this project was abandoned. The existing square dates from the reign of Queen Isabella II (1830–1904). The attractively laid-out gardens contain statues of the kings and queens of Spain, which were originally intended for the top of the Royal Palace facing on to the plaza. They were never put into place because they were too heavy, and Isabella II dreamed that an earthquake caused them to topple onto her.

Teatro Real At the eastern end of the square stands the Royal Theater, built between 1818 and 1850 and now restored. The open-air building that originally occupied the site was expanded in 1737 for a visit by Farinelli, the celebrated castrato singer, of whom Felipe V (1683–1746) was particularly fond.

THE BASICS

- E7
- Plaza de Oriente
- Café de Oriente
- Ópera
- 25

HIGHLIGHT

● The equestrian statue of Felipe IV in the middle of the square is by Montañes, taken from a portrait by Velázquez

TIP

● The Teatro Real is extremely popular and you will need to book well in advance for virtually all performances.

BASILICA DE SAN FRANCISCO EL GRANDE

This 18th-century church has a neoclassical facade by Francisco Sabatini, one of the greatest practitioners of this style, and an overwhelming 33m (108ft) dome. The monastery was used as a barracks from 1835, after which it was lavishly redecorated. The interior (note the ceiling frescoes) contains much work by Spanish masters, including an early Goya, *The Sermon of San Bernadino de Siena,* in the first chapel on the left.

➕ E8 ✉ Plaza de San Francisco, Calle de San Buenaventura 1 ☎ 91 365 38 00 🕐 Sep–Jul Tue–Fri 11–12.30, 4–6.30, Sat 11–1.30; Aug Tue–Sun 11–12.30, 5–7.30 🚇 La Latina 🚌 3, 60, 148 ♿ None 🎟 Inexpensive

CENTRO CULTURAL CONDE DUQUE

condeduquemadrid.es

In 18th-century former barracks with a baroque facade, this dynamic cultural center houses a prestigious contemporary art collection, as well as an auditorium for a regular program of theater, dance and musical performances.

➕ E5 ✉ Conde Duque 9/11 ☎ 91 480 04 01 🚇 Plaza de España, Noviciado 🚌 1, 2, 21, 44, 74, 133 🎟 Free

ESTACIÓN DE PRÍNCIPE PÍO

renfe.com

Aesthetically restored, the former Estación del Norte (North Station) is now both a busy commuter railway station and a lively destination shopping complex (▷ 39). The eye-catching Modernist building was built between 1906 and 1917 by a Valencian architect, hence the typical Valencian details in the facade, including oranges, traditional local costume and La Albufera lake. The station takes its name from Príncipe Pío, the nearby hill, where Spanish rebels were shot by French soldiers on 3 May 1808.

➕ D6 ✉ Paseo de la Florida, corner of Cuesta de San Vicente 🚇 Metro Príncipe Pío 🚌 25, 33, 39, 41, 46, 75, 138

A café on Plaza de España

JARDINES DE LAS VISTILLAS

This park has wonderful views over the Casa de Campo toward the Guadarrama Mountains, as well as several water features, statues and well-maintained flowerbeds. There's a handy café.

🔲 D8 ✉ Travesia Vistillas 🔘 Ópera, La Latina 🚌 3, 148

MURALLA ARABE

What little we can see of the Arab Wall is the oldest surviving part of Madrid. It was originally part of the walls of the small Arab town of Magerit. The area around it, now the Parque Emir Mohammed I, is one of the venues for the popular autumn arts festival.

🔲 D8 ✉ Cuesta de la Vega 🔘 Ópera 🚌 3, 41, 148

PLAZA DE ESPAÑA

A statue of Cervantes stands at the western end of this grandiose square, overlooking a rather lovable 1815 statue of his two legendary creations, Don Quixote and Sancho Panza. On the edge of the square, with a neo-baroque doorway, is the Edificio España, Madrid's first true skyscraper, and the 137m (450ft) Torre Madrid, a symbol of post-Civil War economic recovery and Europe's tallest building when it was built in 1957.

🔲 E6 ✉ Plaza de España 🔘 Plaza de España 🚌 68, 69, 74, 133

SAN NICOLÁS DE LOS SERVITAS

This is Madrid's oldest church and, though much restored after the Civil War, its tower is evidence of the city's Arabic past. The tower is probably the minaret of a mosque later consecrated as a Catholic church. This 12th-century tower is Mudéjar (built by Muslims under Christian rule), while the central apse is Gothic.

🔲 E7 ✉ Plaza de San Nicolás 6 ☎ 91 548 83 14 🕐 Mon 8.30–2, Sun 10–2, 6.30–8.30; do not visit during Mass. Not always open; advance phone call advisable 🔘 Ópera, La Latina

Jardines de las Vistillas

A Walk West from Sol

Stroll through some of Madrid's oldest streets and squares; you will pass plenty of bars and restaurants for a refreshment stop.

DISTANCE: 5km (3 miles) **ALLOW:** 2–3 hours

START

PUERTA DEL SOL
✛ F7 Ⓜ Puerta del Sol

1 Leave the Puerta del Sol at the western end and take Calle de Postas up to Plaza Mayor. Cross the plaza and exit at the diagonally opposite corner (El Arco de los Cuchilleros).

2 At the bottom of the steps cross the street and go down Calle del Maestro de la Villa and into the Plaza Conde de Barajas.

3 Cross the square, turn right on Calle del Conde Miranda, right again on Calle del Codo and into the Plaza de la Villa.

4 Cross Calle Mayor and follow Calle de los Señores de Luzon to the Plaza de Ramales. Cross the square and go downhill to Calle de Lepanto, which leads to the Plaza de Oriente.

END

ARGÜELLES
✛ D5 Ⓜ Argüelles

7 Follow the path around to the right and continue up to the Teleférico. Take a ride for fantastic views or cross Paseo Pintor Rasales and walk up Calle de Marqués Urquijo to Argüelles Metro station.

6 Bear left, following the broad sidewalk to steps leading up the mound to the Templo de Debod. Walk past the temple to admire the views, descend the steps and turn right for the bandstand. Look down the hill to the Rosaleda rose garden.

5 Turn left and walk past the statues to the Palacio Real. Turn right and follow the promenade, walking along the Sabatini Gardens. Do not go down into the tunnel, but climb the steps on the left and continue across the bottom of the Plaza de España.

Shopping

BERBERÍA DEL SAHARA Y EL SAHEL

The name of this shop is a clue: come here for unusual and authentic materials and crafts from North Africa. What makes it different is space devoted to exhibitions, travel guides and other information on the region.

🔢 E8 ✉ Redondilla 8 ☎ 91 354 01 76 🚇 La Latina

CENTRO COMERCIAL PRÍNCIPE PÍO

principepio.es

This conversion of a railway station (the 1881 Estacíon del Norte) is a fine example of the imaginative recycling of old buildings that is going on in Madrid. There are close to 100 shops and boutiques here, including national and international chains, plus places to eat and a multiplex cinema.

🔢 D6 ✉ Paseo de la Florida ☎ 91 758 00 40 🚇 Príncipe Pío

Some outstanding Spanish stores in this shopping complex include:

Massimo Dutti Woman

massimodutti.com

This is an international Spanish company despite its Italian name. Known for its classy style at mid-range prices, this store is devoted to women's clothing, as well as fragrances.

☎ 91 541 08 07

Tino González

tinogonzalez.com

For imaginative yet practical shoes for men, women and children, Tino González has a wide range on offer, from formal to informal—and that special party pair.

☎ 91 632 44 90

FANSI

A classic boutique selling women's fashion from top-flight designers such as Armani and Versace. If this pulls on the purse strings too much, they also carry a sparkling range of evening wear from smaller, lesser-known designers.

🔢 D5 ✉ Calle de la Princesa 74 ☎ 91 543 54 44 🚇 Argüelles

LFONT TEA MOUNTAIN

lfontteamountain.blogspot.com

This enticing small shop sells myriad different teas, plus decorative teapots and mugs, coffees, gift sets, books and some sweet treats, including top-quality chocolates. Enjoy a complimetary drink while you browse.

🔢 E6 ✉ Calle Martin de los Heros 18 ☎ 91 542 50 20 🚇 Plaza de España 🚌 1, 2, 44, 74, 183

MUSEO DEL TRAJE

The Museo del Traje (▷ 31) has one of the best gift shops in the city. It sells a variety of goods but there is a special emphasis on clothing, from delicate Spanish mantillas to elegant silk ties, plus a wonderful jewelry selection.

🔢 C3 ✉ Avenida Juan de Herrera 2 ☎ 91 550 47 00 🚇 Moncloa, Ciudad Universitaria

---

SHOES

Thanks to its centuries-old leather industry, Spain has long had a love affair with *zapatos* (shoes). Many of the world's leading designers are Spanish, mainly from Alicante, Valencia and the Balearic Islands. They range from the extremely expensive (Loewe) to the extremely popular (Camper). Known for its outlet shops with bargain prices is Calle de Augusto Figueroa in Chueca.

Entertainment and Nightlife

LA COQUETTE

This time-tested club is famed for its superb live blues sessions, particularly the legendary Sunday jam sessions. The atmosphere is suitably moodily lit and intimate, with bands performing on a tiny stage.

➕ E7 ✉ Calle Hileras 14 ☎ 91 530 80 95 🕔 Daily from 8pm; shows usually start 10.30 or 11 🚇 Ópera

CORRAL DE LA MORERÍA

corraldelamoreria.com

This legendary flamenco *tablao* restaurant has been going strong for more than 50 years. Reserve ahead.

➕ E8 ✉ Calle de la Morería 17 ☎ 91 365 8446 🕔 Daily from 8pm; shows at 10pm and midnight 🚇 Ópera

GOLEM CINE

golem.es

Originally an art house cinema, Golem still shows international films in original versions with Spanish subtitles. There's also a good basement café.

➕ E6 ✉ Calle Martin de los Heros 14 ☎ 91 559 38 36 🕔 Check for times 🚇 Plaza de España

MARULA CAFÉ

marulacafe.com

Soulfood sessions, hip hop and more draw large crowds to this popular club with DJs and live bands. Party on the outdoor terrace in summer.

➕ E8 ✉ Calle Caños Viejos 3 ☎ 91 366 15 96 🕔 Mon–Sat 11pm–6am 🚇 La Latina

RENOIR

cinesrenoir.com

The best of the cinemas clustered around the bottom of Calle Martín de los Heros shows the latest art films. Detailed information sheets (in Spanish) accompany each one. There are late showings on weekends.

➕ E6 ✉ Calle Martín de los Heros 12 ☎ 91 542 27 02 🚇 Plaza de España

SALA COPÉRNICO

salacopernico.es

Close to the university, this is the place to hear live bands from every part of the spectrum. The decor is themed on a galleon, with telescopes and globes.

➕ E4 ✉ Calle Fernández de los Ríos 67 ☎ 91 562 62 56 🕔 Nightly 11pm–6am 🚇 Moncloa

LAS TABLAS

lastablasmadrid.com

Follow the polka dots to one of the best flamenco shows in the city, with classic performances by accomplished soul-baring dancers and singers. Reserve in advance, particularly on weekends.

➕ E6 ✉ Plaza de España 9 ☎ 91 542 05 20 🕔 Shows daily 8pm and 10pm 🚇 Plaza de España

TEATRO REAL

teatro-real.com

One of the grandest and most beautiful of the European opera houses also stages ballet and classical concerts.

➕ E7 ✉ Plaza de Isabel II ☎ 91 516 06 60/902 24 48 🚇 Ópera

BOOM INDUSTRY

There are at least 60 cinemas in Madrid. Most have a discount day (Monday or Wednesday), when tickets are half price. Always arrive well in advance for evening weekend showings; lines can start forming an hour before projection time. Movie information is published in full in all the daily newspapers: earliest showings (*pasos*) are generally at 4, latest at 10.30.

Where to Eat

LA BOLA (€€)

labola.es

A traditional taberna, La Bola has been in business since 1870, and is still run by the same family. It's best known for its *cocido madrileño* (stew with noodles, chickpeas, meat and vegetables), presented in a sizzling pot. They don't take credit cards.

➕ E7 ✉ Calle de la Bola 5 ☎ 91 547 69 30 🕐 Mon–Sat 1.30–4.30, 8.30–11, Sun 1.30–4.30 🚇 Ópera, Santo Domingo

CAFÉ DE ORIENTE (€€€)

cafedeoriente.es

Built on the remains of a convent and facing the Royal Palace, this is a dress-for-dinner, sophisticated restaurant, with distinctive dishes that fuse *madrileño* and French cuisine.

➕ E7 ✉ Plaza de Oriente 2 ☎ 91 541 39 74 🕐 Daily 8.30am–10.30pm 🚇 Ópera

CASA MINGO (€)

casamingo.es

This popular and atmospheric Asturian *sidrería*, or cider house, is famous for its spit-roasted chicken—and, of course, the cider. Pour it into the glass from a great height and drink it very fast.

➕ C6 ✉ Paseo de la Florida 34 ☎ 91 547 79 18 🕐 Daily 11am–midnight 🚇 Príncipe Pío

CLUB ALLARD (€€€)

elcluballard.com

This Michelin-starred gastronomic treat of a restaurant is appropriately housed in a listed Modernist building. Dishes are beautifully presented and contemporary without being pretentious. The wine pairing for the set menus is carefully selected and excellent.

➕ E6 ✉ Calle Ferraz 2 ☎ 91 559 09 39 🕐 Tue–Sat 1.30–3, 8–10.30 🚇 Plaza de España

DANTXARI (€€–€€€)

dantxari.com

This elegant Basque tavern offers spicy cod, and lamb with garlic and wild mushrooms. There is a wide-ranging Spanish wine list and the service is cheerful and efficient.

➕ E6 ✉ Ventura Rodriguez 8 ☎ 91 542 35 24 🕐 Mon–Sat 1.30–3.30, 8.30–11.30, Sun 1.30–3.30 🚇 Ventura Rodríguez

ENTRE SUSPIRO Y SUSPIRO (€€)

entresuspiroysuspiro.com

Offering a refreshing break from the classical Spanish cuisine that is typical in this area, this Mexican restaurant specializes in well-prepared Mexican dishes, with not a Tex Mex nacho in sight. Reservations are recommended.

➕ E7 ✉ Calle Caños de Peral 3 ☎ 91 420 64 4 🕐 Mon–Sat 2–4, 9–11.30 🚇 Ópera

REGIONAL CUISINE

Spanish regional cusine has achieved greater international recognition than the cuisine of Madrid itself. Basque and Catalan cuisine tends to be fish-based; if you do order meat, it is likely to come in the form of a huge steak. Basque tapas—little culinary works of art—are available at some of the Basque restaurants. Galician specialties include seafood and hearty peasant dishes. The Asturians are known for their cider and *fabadas*, bean-based stews.

EL ESCARPÍN (€€)

elescarpinsidreria.com

Head for the cozy brick-lined dining room for typical Asturian dishes like *fabes con almejas* (white beans with clams) and the famed *fabada Asturiana*, a hearty stew made with white beans, pork shoulder, chorizo and saffron. Asturian cider is the obvious accompanying tipple here.

🔢 E7 ✉ Calle Hileras 17 ☎ 91 559 99 57 🕐 Mon–Thu 9am–12.30am, Fri 9am–2am, Sat 10am–2am 🚇 Ópera

EL INGENIO (€€)

restauranteingenio.com

This restaurant, close to Plaza Santo Domingo, serves traditional Spanish cuisine. The place has a literary feel—Don Quixote paraphernalia adorn the walls. Reserving in advance is advisable, particularly on weekends.

🔢 E6 ✉ Calle de Leganitos 10 ☎ 91 541 91 33 🕐 Mon–Sat 1.30–4, 8.30–midnight, Sun 1.30–4 🚇 Santo Domingo

PRADA A TOPE (€€)

pradaatope.es

Rustic and comfortable, this tavern is enhanced with aged-wood fittings. The cuisine is from León, which is known for its smoked beef, and this restaurant does it well. There are two branches in Madrid—this one and one in Calle del Príncipe in the Centro district.

🔢 D7 ✉ Cuesta de San Vicente 32 ☎ 91 559 39 53 🕐 Daily 12–4.30, 8–midnight 🚇 Plaza de España, Príncipe Pío

SAL GORDA (€€)

restaurantsalgorda.es

This long-established restaurant is off the beaten tourist trail and is very popular with locals for dishes like fried artichokes and hake with clams, and succulent red meats. Servings are generous and the staff are friendly, though they speak limited English.

🔢 E2 ✉ Calle de Beatriz de Bobadilla 9 ☎ 91 553 95 06 🕐 Mon–Sat 1–4, 9–11 🚇 Guzmán el Bueno

SANLÚCAR (€)

Sanlúcar is a classic Andalucian-style tapas bar whose owners are from Cadiz, so a range of sherries are the perfect accompaniment for dishes laden with prawns, *langostinos* (crayfish) and other seafood. Try the well-priced three-course menu of the day.

🔢 E8 ✉ Calle San Isidro Labrador 14 ☎ 91 354 00 52 🕐 Tue–Sat 1–5, 8.30–midnight, Sun 1–5 🚇 La Latina

EL SENADOR (€€)

restaurantesenador.es

This well-established traditional restaurant serves Segovian cuisine. The house special is roast lamb, but there are also steaks cooked on a charcoal fire and fresh fish. The wine is great, and so are the desserts. Tapas are available at the bar. Reserve in advance.

🔢 E7 ✉ Plaza de la Marina Española 2 ☎ 91 541 22 21 🕐 Mon–Sat 1–4, 8.30–midnight, Sun 1–4 🚇 Santo Domingo, Ópera

TABERNA DEL ALABARDERO (€€€)

alabarderomadrid.es

This plush restaurant next to the Teatro Real is named after the soldiers of the king's bodyguard. You're likely to rub shoulders with politicians, bullfighters and literary figures here. If you can't afford the price of a meal, you can enjoy excellent tapas at one of the bar's terrace tables.

🔢 E7 ✉ Calle Felipe V 6 ☎ 91 547 25 77 🕐 Daily 12–11.30 🚇 Ópera

This is the Madrid that most visitors expect to see: medieval lanes, great art museums, and tapas bars on every corner. It's best explored on foot.

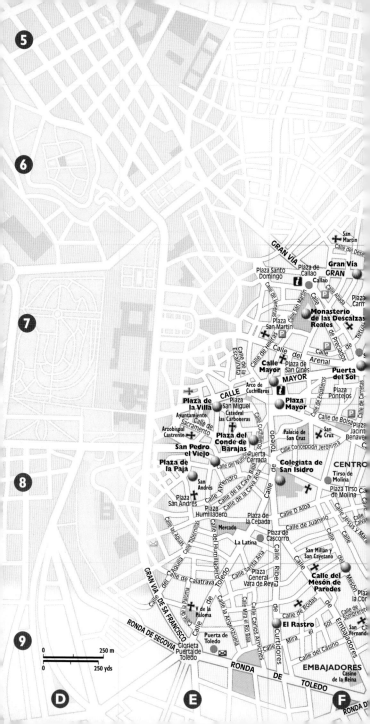

5

6

7

8

9

GRAN VIA

San Martín
Calle del Dese

Plaza Santo
Domingo

Plaza de
Callao

Gran Vía
GRAN

Callao

Calle Alada

Plaza
Carm

Plaza
San Martín

Monasterio
de las Descalzas
Reales

Calle de Tetuán

Calle del
Arenal

Calle de Preciados

Calle
Mayor

Plaza de
San Ginés

MAYOR

Puerta
del Sol

Plaza de
la Villa

CALLE

Plaza
San Miguel
Catedral
las Carboneras

Plaza
Mayor

Arco de
Cuchilleros

Plaza
Pontejos

Plaza
Carretas

Calle de Bolsa

Plaza
Jacinto
Benave

Ayuntamiento

Calle del
Sacramento

Arzobispal
Castrense

Plaza del
Conde de
Barajas

Palacio de
San Cruz

San
Cruz

Calle Concepción Jerónima

CENTRO

San Pedro
el Viejo

Puerta
Cerrada

Colegiata de
San Isidro

Plaza de
la Paja

San
Andrés

Tirso de
Molina

Plaza
San Andrés

Plaza Tirso
de Molina

Plaza
Humilladero

Calle D'Alba

Plaza de
la Cebada

Calle de Juanelo

Calle de Jesús y María

Mercado

La Latina

Plaza de
Cascorro

San Millán y
San Cayetano

GRAN VIA DE SA FRANCISCO

Calle de Calatrava

Y de la
Paloma

Plaza
Santa Ana

Plaza
General
Vara de Rey

Calle del
Mesón de
Paredes

RONDA DE SEGOVIA

Puerta
de Toledo

Glorieta
Puerta de
Toledo

El Rastro

Calle de Rodas

San
Fernando

Calle del Casino

EMBAJADORES
Casino
de la Reina

RONDA

DE

TOLEDO

RONDA D

0   250 m

0   250 yds

D

E

F

Espacio
Fundación
Telefónica

Calle de

las Infantas

Gran Vía

GRAN VÍA

✝ San
José

Calle de la Reina

Calle de Jardines

SOL

Sevilla Calatravas

Calle de la Aduana

ALCALÁ Ministerio
de Educación
Cultura y Deporte

Banco de
España

Real Academia
e Bellas Artes

DE

CALLE

Teatro
Alcázar

Calle de los Madrazo

PASEO DEL PRADO

Calle de Zorilla

Museo
Thyssen-
Bornemisza

ARRERA DE SAN JERÓNIMO

CORTES

Calle de Cervantes

Plaza de
las Cortes

Plaza
Cánovas
del Castillo

Plaza de
Santa Ana

Ateneo

Calle del Prado

laza del
Angel

Calle de Echegaray

Príncipe

Casa Museo
Lope de Vega

Calle de Cervantes

Jesús de
Medinaceli

Plaza
Jesús

Calle
de Atocha

San
Sebastián

Plaza de
Matute

Calle de
León

Calle Lope de Vega

✝ Trinitarias

Calle Santa María

de las Huertas

Plaza de
Antón
Martín

Antón
Martín

Calle de Moratín

Calle de Fúcar

Plaza
Platería
Martínez

e Magdalena

Calle
de la Cabeza

Calle Torrecilla del Leal

Calle del Gobernador

✝

PASEO

DEL

PRADO

Calle del Olmo

Calle

Calle de Almadén

Calle del Olivar

Calle de Ave María

de

Atocha

CaixaForum

Calle de Zurita

Calle de la Fe

Calle del Salitre

Santa

Isabel

INAP

Real Conservatorio
Superior de Música

avapiés Plaza
Lavapiés

Real Monasterio
de Santa Isabel

Calle de Piza

Museo
Nacional
Reina
Sofía

Atocha

Plaza del
Emperador
Carlos V

Calle
Tribulete

Calle San
Lorenzo

de

Argumosa

ATOCHA

Calle
Miguel Servet

Calle

Valencia

Amparo

RONDA

DE

VALENCIA

lorieta de
mbajadores

Embajadores

Teatro
Circo Price

✝ María
Auxiliadora

G   **H**

Museo Nacional Reina Sofía

TOP
25

The splendid modern art collection here concentrates on 20th-century Spanish artists, including Dalí and Miró, though the most famous work here is Picasso's thought-provoking *Guernica*.

A triumph of planning Inspired by the Pompidou Center in Paris, this 12,540sq m (135,000sq ft) space is Madrid's finest contemporary art museum. It occupies a building that served as the San Carlos hospital between 1977 and 1986. Glass elevators on the outside whisk you up for a thrilling view over the rooftops. The permanent collection showcases Spanish art of the 20th century—cubism, surrealism, realism, informalism. The dramatic newer extension is built around a courtyard topped by an eye-catching scarlet metallic roof. This is

Clockwise from far left: The museum's modern facade; Roy Lichtenstein's Brushstroke *(1996) in the courtyard of the Nouvel Building, the museum's extension; close-up of one of the glass elevators; Thomas Schütte's* Imps *(2006) line one of the vaulted corridors running around the central garden*

home to a collection of art dating from the 1960s to the 1980s, exploring themes such as the '68 uprisings, feminism, financial crisis and the growth of popular culture. There's a café-restaurant, bookshop, library and auditorium.

Guernica Picasso's masterpiece dominates the Reina Sofía. When it was commissioned by the Republican Government for display at the 1937 Paris Exhibition, the only instruction was that it be big: it measures 6.4 by 7m (21 by 23ft). Taking his inspiration from the Nationalist bombing of the Basque town of Guernica in 1937, this painting has become 20th-century art's great anti-war symbol. Many saw the 1995 decision to remove the bullet-proof screen that had protected it as a symbolic gesture, showing that democracy in Spain had finally taken root.

THE BASICS

museoreinasofia.es

✚ G9

✉ Calle Santa Isabel 52

☎ 91 774 10 00

🕐 Mon, Wed–Sat 10–9, Sun 10–2.30

🍴 Bar, restaurant

🚇 Atocha

🚉 Atocha

🚌 6, 10, 14, 24, 26, 27, 32, 34, 36, 37, 41, 45, 47, 55, 57, 85, 86

♿ Very good

💵 Moderate. Free to under-18s, over-65s; Sat afternoon and Sun

HIGHLIGHTS

● *Saint Catherine of Alexandria* by Caravaggio
● *Henry VIII* by Holbein
● *Annunciation Diptych* by Van Eyck
● *St. Jerome in the Wilderness* by Titian
● *The Lock* by Constable
● *Last Portrait* by Freud
● *Les Vessenots* by Van Gogh
● *Man with a Clarinet* by Picasso
● *Metropolis* by Grosz
● *Venus and Cupid* by Rubens

TIP

● In summer, the rooftop terrace is open for romantic dinners. Also in summer, the museum is open late at night.

This eclectic art collection contains works from a huge range of leading Western artists, from Renaissance greats such as Caravaggio to edgy contemporary painters such as Lucian Freud.

Background The collection was begun by the German financier and industrialist Baron Heinrich Thyssen-Bornemisza in the 1920s and continued after his death by his son, Hans Heinrich (who died in 2002). The 775 paintings exhibited here were sold to the Spanish state for a mere $350 million in 1993, one year after the museum opened to the public. The permanent collection, spanning seven centuries, is housed in the sympathetically renovated 18th-century Palacio de Villahermosa. The glass pavilion contains 19th- and 20th-century

From left: The museum's spacious entrance hall; abstract and figurative art gallery displaying Richard Lindner's Thank You *(1971)*

paintings from the collection of Hans Heinrich's widow, Carmen Thyssen-Bornemisza, a former Miss Spain.

The collection The sheer variety of the many works on display prompted some to call the Thyssen over-eclectic; others claim its very quirkiness is part of its charm. Each room highlights a different period: the top floor is devoted to art from medieval times through to the 17th century; the second floor to rococo and neoclassicism through to fauvism and expressionism; the first level to 20th-century surrealism, pop art and the avant-garde. Start from the top and work your way down. It is definitely worth renting an audio guide. The museum's shop is one of the best, whether you are looking for art books or beautiful gifts.

THE BASICS

museothyssen.org

✚ G7

✉ Paseo del Prado 8

☎ 902 76 05 11

🕐 Tue–Sun 10–7, Mon 12–4

🍴 Café, restaurant

🚉 Atocha, Recoletos

Ⓜ Banco de España

🚌 1, 2, 5, 9, 10, 14, 15, 20, 27, 34, 37, 45, 51, 52, 53, 74, 146, 150

♿ Excellent

💶 Expensive. Free to children under 12; reduction to over-65s. Free Mon 12–4

Monasterio de las Descalzas Reales

TOP
25

Marble tomb of the Empress Maria (left) at the Monasterio de las Descalzas Reales (right)

THE BASICS

patrimonionacional.es
🔂 F7
✉ Plaza de las Descalzas Reales 3
☎ 91 454 88 00
🕐 Tue–Sat 10–2, 4–6.30, Sun 10–3
🚇 Sol, Ópera
🚌 3, 25, 39, 148
♿ None
💷 Moderate

HIGHLIGHTS

● *Recumbent Christ* by Gaspar Becerra
● *Neapolitan Nativity* (Chapel of St. Michael)
● *Bust of the Mater Dolorosa* by José Risueño
● *Cardinal Infante Don Fernando of Austria* by Rubens
● *The Ship of the Church*, 16th-century painting
● *Adoration of the Magi* by Brueghel
● *The Empress María* by Goya
● 17th-century tapestries

A working convent to this day, the Monastery of the Barefoot Royal Ladies contains a stunning collection of tapestries, paintings and sculptures, as well as other priceless treasures, yet it remains one of the city's lesser known top sights.

Convent history Of Madrid's two monastery museums (the other is Monasterio de la Encarnación, ▷ 27), the Descalzas Reales is the richer; most of its rooms are museums in themselves. With its incongruous location right in the middle of commercial Madrid, it is a small miracle that the convent remains intact. It was founded by Juana of Austria, the younger daughter of Carlos V, on the site of the place in which she was born, and built between 1559 and 1564 in Madrid brick. The whole place breathes mid-17th-century religious mysticism, though the "vile stink" of which traveler William Beckford complained when attending Mass in the late 18th century has gone. The original sisters were all of noble or aristocratic blood, and each founded a chapel on reception into the order: there are 33 of them, and to this day the convent is home to 23 Franciscan nuns, each of whom maintains at least one of the chapels.

Seeing the collection The only way to see the convent is to take a tour. Given in Spanish and English, it lasts around 45 minutes and is conducted fairly speedily so it is worth buying a guide book at the entrance. The church can be visited only during Mass, at 8am or 7pm.

Views of the Casa de Panadería on Plaza Mayor

TOP
25

Plaza Mayor

Plaza Mayor is the historic central hub of Madrid. It is an architectural splendor, flanked by sumptuous 18th-century buildings and two pinnacle towers, and lined with sidewalk cafés.

Work in progress Built in the 15th century as a market square, the Plaza Mayor came into its own when Felipe II, after making Madrid the capital of Spain, ordered it to be rebuilt as his administrative center. The only part to be completed immediately was the Panadería, or the bakery, in 1590 (the frescoes date from the early 1990s), while the rest of it was finished in 1619 under Felipe III, whose bronze statue stands in the middle. After a fire in 1790, much of the square was rebuilt. The buildings between the towers on either side are Town Hall offices; the rest are private homes. The 18th-century Arco de los Cuchilleros, leading from the square into Cava Baja, is named after the cutlers who worked here, making knives for local butchers and swords for the nobility.

A gathering place During the 17th century, the more important members of the court lived here; at the end of the century, the square became the site of mounted bullfights, carnivals and the terrible *autos da fé* of the Spanish Inquisition, which were attended by thousands. On 30 June 1680, 118 offenders were executed in a single day. Today the plaza bustles with tourists and locals, and on Sundays hosts a popular stamp and coin market.

THE BASICS
✚ F7/8
✉ Plaza Mayor
🍴 *Terraza* bars around square
Ⓜ Sol, Ópera
🚌 3, 17, 18, 23, 31, 35
❓ Tourist office in square

TIPS
● In May, free concerts are held during the 2 May and San Isidro festivities.
● The plaza hosts the city's annual Christmas market.
● Restaurants and bars in the plaza tend to be pricey.

CENTRO TOP 25

Plaza de la Paja

The old bishop's palace, Palacio Vargas (left); 1997 bronze statue of man reading a newspaper (right)

THE BASICS

- ✚ E8
- ✉ Plaza de la Paja
- ⏱ Jardín del Principe Anglona: May–Sep daily 10–10; Oct–Apr daily 10–6
- Ⓜ La Latina
- 🚌 3, 31, 148

HIGHLIGHTS

- ● Bishop's Palace
- ● San Andrés church
- ● Capilla de Opispo
- ● Capilla de San Isidro
- ● Jardín del Principe Anglona

One of the oldest squares in Madrid, this charming plaza was once part of the Morería area, where the city's Mudéjar Muslims were confined for four centuries. Today, it's a popular meeting place.

History After the Muslims were driven out of Madrid in the 11th century by Alfonso VI of León and Castile, Plaza de la Paja became the civic and commercial center of Madrid before the construction of the far grander Plaza Mayor in the 17th century. The plaza's name (Straw Square) is derived from the days when it was a grain and fodder market for the chaplain's and bishop's mules. The 16th-century former bishop's palace at the north end of the square has a striking Renaissance facade. Other noteworthy buildings that survived the 19th-century reconstruction of the plaza include the baroque church of San Andrés and the neighboring chapel of San Isidro.

Present day One of the delights of the square is that it is pedestrianized, offering a tranquil respite for a drink or meal right in the bustling center of the city. As well as the bars and cafés, there are shady plane trees, benches and a couple of sculptures that really capture the laid-back feel of the place. The square also includes an access to one of the few examples of 18th-century walled gardens remaining in Madrid: the Jardín del Principe Anglona is a delightful formal garden with fountains, walkways and rose beds.

The bear and tree, symbol of Madrid (left); statue of Carlos III (middle and right)

TOP **25**

Puerta del Sol

A main transportation hub in the city, Puerta del Sol is considered the heart and soul of Madrid by many inhabitants. Each year thousands gather here to see in the New Year.

Soul of Madrid The area's namesake gateway was demolished in 1570 when the square was widened to receive Anne of Austria, Felipe II's fourth wife. The design of the present square dates back to 1861; the building on the south side, the Casa de Correos, is from 1768. Originally the Post Office, it is now the headquarters of the Madrid regional government. Spain's Kilometer Zero, the point from which all distances in Spain are measured, can be found on the pavement in front of it.

A troubled past The Esquilache mutiny of 1766 began here, sparked by Carlos III's uncharacteristically tyrannical insistence that the population should wear short capes and three-cornered hats to emulate a hated French style. The most notable moment in Sol's history was on 2 and 3 May 1808, when *madrileños* took up arms against occupying French troops, a heroic resistance in which more than 2,000 died, immortalized in Goya's two magnificent anti-war paintings in the Prado, *Dos de Mayo* and *Tres de Mayo*. It was here, also, that the Second Republic was proclaimed in 1931. It remains a popular meeting place, especially by the monument of the bear with a strawberry tree, the symbol of Madrid.

THE BASICS

✚ F7
✉ Puerta del Sol
Ⓢ Sol
🚌 3, 5, 15, 20, 51, 52, 150

HIGHLIGHTS

● Bear and *madroño* (strawberry tree) statue
● Statue of Carlos III
● La Mallorquina pastry shop
● Newspaper stands: a major part of Madrid streetlife
● Tío Pepe sign
● Kilometer Zero
● Doña Manolita's lottery ticket kiosk

CENTRO TOP 25

El Rastro

Grab a bargain at El Rastro market— or at least have fun looking

THE BASICS

elrastro.org

🚇 F9

✉ Ribera de Curtidores

🕐 8–2.30

🍴 Many cafés and bars

🚇 Tirso de Molina

HIGHLIGHTS

● Street vendors shouting
● Spanish pottery
● Antiques at Galerías Piquer
● Leather boots and saddles at Curtidos Roman riding shop, Calle Ribera de Curtidores 16

TIP

Be extra careful with your valuables in the throng.

For locals and visitors alike, this is the classic place to spend a leisurely Sunday morning. The Rastro is much more than a flea market; it is a vibrant, noisy, invigorating experience that has been a Madrid experience for over 50 years.

Bargains galore Start from the Tirso de Molina Metro station, and head for the Plaza de Cascorro. The lines of stalls run downhill, along both sides and through the middle of the Ribera de Curtidores street, to form a busy triangle with Calle de Toledo and Calle Embajadores. It all gets underway at 9am. The trick is to take your time and tuck all your valuables away. Bargains are here for those who poke, prod and haggle for old birdcages, cheap underwear, leather bags and clay pots.

A bloody history The shopping experience is not limited to just the main street. All the regular shops are open, and the market spills into the side streets. Find pets (spcecifically birds) on Calle de Fray Ceferino González, and every sort of painting, from watercolors and prints to original oils, on the Calle de San Cayetano, nicknamed the Painters' Street. Drop by the Galerías Piquér (▷ 62), a courtyard surrounded by antiques shops. As for the name, *rastro* dates back to the 16th century, when this was the site of a slaughterhouse. When the dead animals were dragged away to the tanners (*curtidores*), they left a *rastro*, trail of blood, on the street.

Graceful facade of the Royal Academy of Fine Arts

Real Academia de Bellas Artes

The Royal Academy of Fine Arts has a rich and eclectic collection, ranging from 13 works by Goya to exquisite and little-known Picasso engravings. It is the oldest permanent art institution in Madrid.

History Work began on the Academy under the authorization of Felipe V in 1744 and was completed under Fernando VI in 1752. The original building was baroque, but shortly after it opened, Academy members with conservative tastes insisted that it be given today's neoclassical facade. This museum is rarely overcrowded and it is small enough to be visited comfortably in a couple of hours.

Layout The museum has three floors. Many of its most famous paintings are on the second floor, most notably Room 20, with its works by Goya, including two poignant self-portraits and the renowned *El Entierro de la Sardina* (*Burial of the Sardine*). Other highlights by 17th-century Spanish artists include *Head of John the Baptist* by José de Ribera (1591–1652) and *Alonso Rodríguez* by Francisco Zurbarán. *Spring,* the whimsical surrealistic portrait of a man made up entirely of flowers, by the 16th-century Milanese painter Giuseppe Arcimboldo, is in Room 14; it's the only Arcimboldo in Spain and one of only a handful in the world. The Calcografía Nacional, or Engravings Museum, contains the Gabinete Goya, with a beautifully displayed series of the original plates used by the artist for his etchings.

THE BASICS

realacademiabellasartes-sanfernando.com

➕ G7

✉ Calle de Alcalá 13

☎ 91 524 08 64

🕐 Tue–Sun 10–3

Ⓜ Sol, Sevilla

🚌 3, 5, 15, 20, 51, 52, 53, 150

♿ Limited

💲 Moderate. Free to under-18s, over-65s

HIGHLIGHTS

● Goya self-portraits (Room 20)
● *The Burial of the Sardine* by Goya (Room 20)
● *Alonso Rodríguez* by Francisco Zurbarán (Room 6)
● *Head of John the Baptist* by José de Ribera (Room 3)
● *Felipe IV* by Velázquez (Room 11)
● *Susana and the Elders* by Rubens (Room 13)
● *Spring* by Giuseppe Arcimboldo (Room 14)
● Goya etchings

TIP

● Don't miss the Calcografía Nacional, with its room full of Goya's disturbing engravings.

More to See

CAIXAFORUM

caixaforum.es

This exhibition space and concert hall is an extraordinary piece of architecture. The former power station now has an angular red extension sprouting from its roof, and the entrance is so recessed that the whole building looks as though it is hovering above the ground. What would otherwise be an ugly bare wall in front of the entrance has been transformed into a "vertical garden", a mass of dripping greenery.

➕ H8 ✉ Paseo del Prado 36 ☎ 91 330 73 00 🕐 Daily 10–8 Ⓜ Atocha 🚌 10, 14, 27, 34, 45 ♿ Good 💷 Inexpensive; occasional charge for certain concerts

CALLE MAYOR

This is perhaps the most traditional of Madrid's streets, with some old-fashioned shops—including a wonderful *guitarrería* (guitar store) near the Calle Bailén end. Two of Spain's greatest playwrights, Lope de Vega and Calderón de la Barca, lived at Nos. 25 and 61 respectively. The latter is easy to miss as the facade is only 4m (13ft) wide!

➕ E/F7 Ⓜ Sol 🚌 3

CALLE DEL MESÓN DE PAREDES

To get a sense of the multicultural atmosphere of Madrid's *barrio popular* in Lavapiés, stroll down this street and those around it on a weekday morning, when it is bustling and full of life. La Corrala is an 1882 example of the corridor tenement found throughout working-class Madrid. From the early 1980s, it was used as an open-air theater and is now an official Artistic Monument. The Taberna de Antonio Sánchez at No. 13 (▷ 66) is one of the best-preserved examples of Madrid's traditional 19th-century bars. A few others survive around the old parts of the city, some of them with their original tile work and polished zinc counters.

➕ F9 Ⓜ Tirso de Molina, Lavapiés 🚌 32, 57

Gran Vía

CASA MUSEO LOPE DE VEGA

casamuseolopedevega.org

Spain's greatest playwright, Felix Lope de Vega (1562–1635), lived in this house from 1610 until his death. Now an evocative museum, the rooms are furnished in the style of the period, based on an inventory by Lope himself. There are lovely gardens behind the museum, which you will find just uphill from the Paseo.

➕ G8 ✉ Calle de Cervantes 11 ☎ 91 429 92 16 🕐 Tue–Sun 10–3 🚇 Banco de España, Antón Martín 🚌 On Paseo del Prado ♿ Poor 🎫 Free

COLEGIATA DE SAN ISIDRO

San Isidro is the patron saint of Madrid and, between 1885 and 1993, until the completion of the Almudena (▷ 25), this immense baroque church was Madrid's unofficial cathedral. Built in 1620 by Pedro Sánchez for the Jesuits, the church was commandeered by Carlos III after he expelled them. San Isidro's remains, until then in the nearby church of San Andrés, were brought here at that time.

➕ F8 ✉ Calle Colegiata 17 ☎ 91 369 20 37 🕐 Daily 7–1.30, 5–9 🚇 Tirso de Molina, La Latina 🚌 3, 6, 17, 18, 23, 26, 32, 50, 60, 148 ♿ None 🎫 Free

ESPACIO FUNDACIÓN TELEFÓNICA

espacio.fundaciontelefonica.com

Occupying four floors within the historic Telefónica building, the permanent exhibitions here include an insightful look at the history of telecommunications, right up to the latest smartphone technology and the Facebook-Instagram revolution. There is also a pleasant café.

➕ F7 ✉ Calle Fuencarral 3 ☎ 91 580 87 00 🕐 Tue–Sun 10–8 🚇 Gran Vía 🚌 1, 2, 46, 74, 146, 202 ♿ Good 🎫 Free

GRAN VÍA

Running between the Calle de Alcalá and the Plaza de España, the massive Gran Vía is one of the city's great axes; with its shops and cinemas, it is lively and stimulating for

A portrait of Lope de Vega at his former home, Casa Museo Lope de Vega

early evening strolls. Conceived in the late 19th century as a way to allow Madrid to expand, it led to the shortening or destruction of 54 other streets. Serving as Madrid's great northern axis, the road peels off from Calle de Alcalá a short way from Plaza de Cibeles. Work finally began in 1910 under Alfonso XII and was completed in 1929. The building of this thoroughfare provided an opportunity for architects of the early 20th century to apply new styles. The best are at the start of the street, on or near the junction of Alcalá and the Gran Vía. The most striking building is the Metropolis, which was finished in 1911. Its slate dome is ornamented with gold and topped by a winged statue of Victory. Next to it is No. 1 Gran Vía, the Edificio Grassy (1917), named after the jeweler's shop on the first floor and distinguished by its colonnaded tower. Moving up the street, on the north side (No. 12) is a 1931 art deco cocktail bar, Museo Chicote, made

famous by its association with author Ernest Hemingway and the Hollywood actress Ava Gardner. Don't miss the Telefónica building (No. 28), a Manhattan-style skyscraper, the tallest building in Madrid when it was erected in 1929, which now houses the telecommunications museum (▷ 57).

🚇 F/G7 🚇 Gran Vía, Callao 🚌 44, 46, 74, 133, 146, 147, 148, 149

PLAZA DEL CONDE DE BARAJAS

Looking for a special souvenir of Madrid? Visit this delightful spot on a Sunday, when artists set up their stalls to sell oil paintings and watercolors. Prices range from cheap to unbelievably high, but it is worth haggling. At Christmas, concerts and flamenco dancing events are also held here. It's located southwest of the Plaza Mayor, between Calle de la Pasa and the Pasadizo del Panecillo.

🚇 E8 🚇 La Latína

Congreso de los Diputados on Plaza de las Cortes

Plaza del Conde de Barajas

PLAZA DE LAS CORTES

congreso.es

This is the home of the Congreso de los Diputados, or parliament buildings. The ceremonial entrance to the parliament is guarded by two bronze lions popularly known as Daoíz and Velarde after the heroic captains of the Dos de Mayo uprising against the French. An attempted military coup took place inside the building in 1981, and was recorded on video for posterity. There are weekly guided tours. In the middle of the square stands a statue of Spain's most famous author, Miguel de Cervantes (1547–1616), renowned for his novel *Don Quixote*.

➕ G7 ✉ Plaza de las Cortes 🚇 Sevilla 🚌 5, 150, N5, N6

PLAZA DE SANTA ANA

Once occupied by the Santa Ana monastery, which was torn down during Joseph Bonaparte's rule (1808–13), the refurbished plaza is now surrounded by bars, making it the perfect spot for people-watching in summer. The square is also home to the oldest theater in Madrid, Teatro Español. Built in 1745, it puts on classical Spanish productions.

➕ F8 ✉ Plaza de Santa Ana 🚇 Sol, Sevilla 🚌 5, 150

PLAZA DE LA VILLA

With its small scale, this rectangular and typically Castilian square makes a pleasant change from some of the more imposing buildings in Madrid. Originally the site of an Arab street market, it is now home to three buildings in three distinct styles: the Castilian-baroque Ayuntamiento, the Casa de la Villa, designed in 1630 by Juan Gómez de Mora; the much-restored Casa de Cisneros, on the south side of the square, one of Madrid's finest examples of the plateresque style prevalent in the 16th century; and the Torre de los Lujanes, one of the city's few surviving monuments from the 15th century.

➕ E8 ✉ Plaza de la Villa 🚇 Sol, Ópera 🚌 3

SAN PEDRO EL VIEJO

Noteworthy principally for its 14th-century Mudéjar tower and the legends surrounding it, San Pedro stands on the site of an old mosque. In the doorway are the only coats of arms extant from the period preceding the Catholic monarchs. Part of the interior dates from the 15th century, while the rest is largely of 18th-century construction.

➕ E8 ✉ Calle Nuncio 14 ☎ 91 365 12 84 🕐 Daily 6–8pm; do not visit during Mass 🚇 La Latina, Tirso de Molina 🚫 None

Casa de Guadalajara, Plaza de Santa Ana

A Walk East from Sol

Take this walk to see the Spanish parliament and the Prado, the Botanic Gardens and Retiro Park.

DISTANCE: 6.7km (4 miles) **ALLOW**: 2–3 hours

START

PUERTA DEL SOL
🚇 F7 🚌 Puerta del Sol

1 Start on the Puerta del Sol. Exit at its eastern end and walk down Calle de San Jerónimo, all the way to the Plaza de las Cortes. Continue past the south side of the Museo Thyssen-Dornemisza to the Plaza de Cánovas de Castillo.

2 Turn right down the Paseo del Prado and cross at Plaza de la Platería de Martínez. Visit the Jardín Botánico, on the south side of the Prado, or continue along Calle de Espalter to Calle de Moreto.

3 Turn left and walk uphill, past San Jerónimo del Real, to Calle de Félipe IV. Turn right, walk up past the Casón del Buen Retiro, cross Calle de Alfonso XII and enter the Retiro Park.

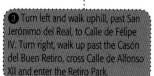

END

CALLE DE ALCALÁ
🚇 G7 🚌 Banco de España

7 Continue past the Plaza de las Silesa and turn sharp left down Calle de Barquillo. Follow this all the way down to Calle de Alcalá.

6 At the Plaza de Colón, turn left on Paseo de Recoletos. Cross over at the entrance to Recoletos station. On the west side of the Paseo, turn right on Calle Bárbara de Braganza.

5 At the fountain, bear left for the Puerta de Alcalá, cross Calle de Alcalá, and walk up Calle de Serrano. Pass the Archaeological Museum and turn left on Calle de Jorge Juan.

4 Stroll through the parterre gardens and up the steps at the end. When you reach the lake, turn left and follow its edge. Across the water you will see the dramatic Alfonso XII monument.

Shopping

AMPARO MERCERÍA

As this grand old haberdashery store confirms, stitching and mending, sewing and knitting are ever popular in Spain. Founded back in 1861, the store retains that sense of history with a solid wood counter, as well as selections of buttons, needles, sequins and lace.

F7 ✉ Calle Marqués Viudo de Pontejos 5 ☎ 91 521 98 08 🚇 Sol

ANTIGUA CASA TALAVERA

antiguacasatalavera.com

Talavera, Granada and Toledo are known for fine, hand-painted ceramics, and this 100-year-old establishment has both original and reproduction pieces with patterns that go back 1,000 years.

E7 ✉ Calle de Isabel la Católica 2 ☎ 91 547 34 17 🚇 Santo Domingo

ANTIGUA PASTELERÍA DEL POZO

This bakery dates back to 1830 and is known for its *roscones de Reyes*, a sweet bread associated with the Three Kings festival (6 January). Happily, these rings of brioche-style bread, dotted with sugar and glazed fruits, are made on the premises year-round. Alternatively, go for the delicious tarts filled with pumpkin jam (*cabello de ángel*) and custard.

F7 ✉ Calle Pozo 8 ☎ 91 522 38 94 🚇 Sol

CASA DE DIEGO

casadediego.info

This 150-year-old store is still the best place in Madrid to buy a real fan. They range from cheap and cheerful versions to exquisite hand-painted collector's items. The shop also sells umbrellas and walking sticks.

F9 ✉ Plaza de la Puerta del Sol 12 ☎ 91 522 66 43 🚇 Sol

EL CORTE INGLÉS

elcorteingles.es

Spain's pride and joy, this department store sells everything, and ensures good value for money. There are some 20 branches in Madrid, including this flagship store on Calle de Preciados, just off the Puerta del Sol.

F7 ✉ Calle de Preciados 1 ☎ 91 379 80 00 🚇 Sol

LA FAVORITA

lafavoritacb.com

The oldest hat shop in the city, Favorita was founded here on the Plaza Mayor back in 1894. Today it sells all types of modern head gear, including caps (*gorras*) and berets.

F7 ✉ Plaza Mayor 25 ☎ 91 366 58 77 🚇 Sol

FELIX ANTIGÜEDADES

In the heart of the Rastro flea market you'll find an intriguing collection of objects, especially Oriental art and musical instruments, in this antiques shop.

F9 ✉ Plaza General Vara del Rey 3 ☎ 91 365 60 98 🚇 La Latina

EL FLAMENCO VIVE

elflamencovive.com

There is no doubt that flamenco lives inside Alberto Martínez's shop, which is entirely devoted to flamenco. In addition to a good selection of music, there are books and flamenco paraphernalia.

E7 ✉ Calle Conde de Lemos 7 ☎ 91 547 39 17 🚇 Opera

FNAC

fnac.es

There are five floors of books and CDs, plus a small concert area. Also has foreign newspapers, photograph developing services and a ticket agency.

🚇 F7 ✉ Calle de Preciados 28 ☎ 90 210 06 32 Ⓜ Callao

GALERÍAS PIQUÉR

This pleasant mall in the Rastro street market has 20 antiques shops. Try Siglo 20 for art deco, and El Estudio for Isabelline furniture and lamps.
🚇 F9 ✉ Calle Ribera de Curtidores 29 Ⓜ La Latina, Rastro

GIL

This small shop specializes in exquisitely embroidered traditional Spanish shawls and *mantillas* (veils), which are still worn on special occasions, as well as hand-painted fans.
🚇 F7 ✉ Carrera de San Jerónimo 2 ☎ 91 521 25 49 Ⓜ Sol

GUANTES LUQUE

There's a vast range of gloves, with prices to suit every pocket, at this 150-year-old store. Gloves come in wool, leather, cotton and silk, in myriad colors, for every occasion and every season of the year.
🚇 E8 ✉ Calle Espoz y Mina 3, Santa Ana ☎ 91 522 32 87 Ⓜ La Latina

GUITARRAS RAMÍREZ

guitarrasramirez.com
Since 1882, four generations of the Ramírez family have made and sold some of Spain's finest guitars, which have been bought by amateurs as well as world-famous professional musicians (including John Lennon) from around the globe.
🚇 F8 ✉ Calle de la Paz 8 ☎ 91 531 42 29 Ⓜ Sol

MARÍA CABELLO

Dating from 1913 with an original frieze ceiling, this enticing shop specializes in fine local wines. The friendly owner can advise you and speaks some English.
🚇 G7 ✉ Calle de Echegaray 5 ☎ 91 429 60 88 Ⓜ Sol

MARIANO MADRUEÑO

marianomadrueno.es
The Spanish drink a wide range of their own wines, as well as liqueurs such as *pacharán* (sloe gin). Barrels and alembics decorate this century-old wine shop near the Monasterio de las Descalzas Reales. It's still run by the same family and you will find the staff helpful.
🚇 F7 ✉ Calle Postigo de San Martín 3 ☎ 91 521 19 55 Ⓜ Callao

SESEÑA

sesena.com
With a firm eye on maintaining quality, this family establishment, dating back to 1901, specializes in capes. Pablo Picasso, Victoria Beckham and Hillary Clinton have all been customers.
🚇 F7/8 ✉ Calle de la Cruz 23 ☎ 91 531 68 40 Ⓜ Sol

LA VIOLETA

lavioletaonline.es
This tiny shop could be out of a fairy tale. It specializes in an unusual sweet: real sugared violets in jars and pretty little boxes. It also sells chocolates and candied fruits, and everything is wrapped beautifully.
🚇 F7 ✉ Plaza de Canalejas 6 ☎ 91 522 55 22 Ⓜ Sol

> ### SHOPPING AROUND
>
> Try to explore the back streets of Madrid, where you will find small, independent shops. They tend to close from about 1.30 to about 4.30, although larger stores and malls are open through lunch.

Entertainment and Nightlife

ARCO DE CUCHILLEROS

Top dancers and singers have performed here for nearly 50 years. It is more like a bar with entertainment than a club, so have a drink and watch the action between 9pm and 2am.

🟦 E8 ✉ Calle Cuchilleros 7 ☎ 91 364 02 63 🕐 Closed Mon 🚇 Sol

BERLIN CABARET 1930

berlincabaret.com

The Spanish love magic tricks, as well as the usual risqué song and dance, drag shows and high-kicking chorus lines. Expect lots of red velvet and a happy crowd. Shows at this café-theater often start as late as 1am.

🟦 E8 ✉ Costanilla de San Pedro 11 ☎ 91 366 20 34 🕐 Closed Mon 🚇 La Latina, Ópera

CAFÉ CENTRAL

cafecentralmadrid.com

One of the best jazz venues in Europe, the Central has performances every night, mainly from Spanish, but sometimes foreign, musicians.

🟦 F8 ✉ Plaza del Ángel 10 ☎ 91 369 41 43 🕐 Daily 10.30pm 🚇 Sevilla, Antón Martín, Sol

CAFÉ POPULART

The Populart offers live music every day—jazz, blues and swing—in a great environment with lively conversation.

🟦 G8 ✉ Calle Huertas 22 ☎ 91 429 84 07 🚇 Antón Martín

LAS CARBONERAS

tablaslascarboneras.com

Madrid's main flamenco club is rated by aficionados for its quality acts. The show begins around 11pm, but arrive earlier if you want to be sure of a seat.

🟦 E8 ✉ Calle del Conde de Miranda 1 ☎ 91 542 86 77 🚇 Sol

CARDAMOMO

cardamomo.com

This flamenco show venue is a well-respected and long-established. It's more authentic than most and attracts Spaniards as well as international tourists. The admission price includes a drink.

🟦 G7 ✉ Calle de Echegaray 15 ☎ 91 369 07 57 🕐 Shows daily from 6pm 🚇 Sol

CASA PATAS

casapatas.com

The best-known of Madrid's flamenco shows is a little touristy, but none the less enjoyable. There are live midnight performances, more frequent in May.

🟦 F8 ✉ Calle Cañizares 10 ☎ 91 369 15 74/04 96 🕐 Performances Thu–Sat midnight 🚇 Tirso de Molina, Antón Martín

CERVECERÍA ALEMANA

cerveceriaalemana.com

One of the city's most popular bars, Alemana is a good meeting place in the Santa Ana district.

🟦 F8 ✉ Plaza de Santa Ana 6 ☎ 91 429 70 33 🚇 Antón Martín

CINE DORÉ

mecd.gob.es

A restored old cinema is now the seat of Filmoteca Española, the national film institute. Most of the films shown are in their original language with subtitles in Spanish. Even when there's nothing on, it has a good bar-restaurant and bookshop.

🟦 G8 ✉ Santa Isabel 3 ☎ 91 369 11 25 🚇 Antón Martín

LE COCK

Round off the evening with a cocktail or two beneath the glass roof of this tastefully decorated late-night bar.

🕀 G7 ✉ Calle Reina 16 ☎ 91 532 28 26
🚇 Banco de España

GLASS BAR

hotelurban.com
This bar in the lobby of the Hotel Urban, named for its shiny glass decor, offers expensive cocktails, chill-out music and innovative tapas.
🕀 G7 ✉ Carrera de San Jerónimo 34
🕐 Daily 11am–3am ☎ 91 787 77 70 🚇 Sol, Antón Martín

JOY ESLAVA

joy-eslava.com
Plush, though not forbiddingly stylish, this club occupies an 1850s theater. The central location attracts a diverse clientele for equally diverse entertainment, ranging from latino nights to live acts and cabarets.
🕀 F7 ✉ Calle Arenal 11 ☎ 91 366 37 33
🚇 Ópera

SALA EL SOL

salaelsol.com
Things start happening at El Sol around midnight and the pace gets faster and faster through til 5am. Pay the €12 entry—which includes a drink—and dance to a mix of R'n'B, soul, funk and rock; great atmosphere, great people, and no frills.
🕀 F7 ✉ Calle Jardines 3 ☎ 91 532 64 90
🚇 Gran Via, Sol

TEATRO MONUMENTAL

rtve.es
Classical concerts are recorded in this former movie theater for broadcast by the Spanish Radio and Televison Orchestra and Choir. Concerts are mostly on Fridays.
🕀 G8 ✉ Calle Atocha 65 ☎ 91 429 12 81
🚇 Antón Martín

TEATRO DE LA ZARZUELA

teatrodelazarzuela.mcu.es
Zarzuela, or light opera, is particularly popular with the older generation in Madrid. Even if you don't speak Spanish, the farcical plots are simple and easy to understand. The music and singing are top class. Enjoy it at this 150-year-old theater.
🕀 G7 ✉ Jovellanos 4 ☎ 91 524 54 00
🕐 Check schedule 🚇 Antón Martín

TORRES BERMEJAS

torresbermejas.com
For over 45 years, this restaurant and club has hosted some of the most famous flamenco singers and dancers in the world. The setting is reminiscent of the Alhambra palace in Granada. Eat traditional Spanish dishes and then enjoy the show.
🕀 F7 ✉ Mesonero Romanos 11 ☎ 91 532 33 22 🚇 Callao

VIVA MADRID

vivamadrid.com
The tiled *azulejo* frontage of Viva Madrid bar has been photographed for a thousand guide books. Step within, and the classic tiled decor is similarly striking, accentuated by a traditional vaulted ceiling.
🕀 G8 ✉ Calle Manuel Fernández y González 7 ☎ 91 429 36 40 🚇 Antón Martín

ZARZUELA

In the words of Edmundo de Amici, writing in 1870, the *zarzuela,* or light opera, is "a piece of music somewhere between comedy and melodrama, between opera and vaudeville, with prose and verse, both recited and sung, serious and light-hearted, a very Spanish and very entertaining musical form".

Where to Eat

PRICES
Prices are approximate, based on a 3-course meal for one person.
€€€   over €60
€€   €35–€60
€   under €35

BOTÍN (€€)

botin.es

Botín first opened its doors in 1725, making it, according to the *Guinness Book of Records*, the world's oldest restaurant. Goya worked here as a waiter. Suckling pig, roasted in a wood-fired oven, is the special.

🞤 E8 ✉ Calle Cuchilleros 17 ☎ 91 366 42 17 🕓 Daily 1–4, 8–midnight 🚇 La Latina

LOS CARACOLES (€)

How authentic do you want? This is all about snails: casseroled, with lots of garlic. Wash them down with a glass of draft vermouth. Eat standing up and feel like a local.

🞤 E9 ✉ Plaza Cascorro ☎ 91 365 94 39 🕓 Tue–Sat 9am–11pm, Sun till 7.30pm 🚇 Puerta de Toledo

CASA ALBERTO (€€)

casaalberto.es

Founded in 1827, this characterful restaurant is at the back of a bar that serves terrific tapas. Bullfighting memorabilia, wood paneling and hanging hams complete the picture.

🞤 G8 ✉ Calle de las Huertas 18 ☎ 91 429 93 56 🕓 Tue–Sat 1.30–4, 8–midnight, Sun 1.30–4 🚇 Antón Martin

CASA LABRA (€€)

casalabra.es

The Spanish Socialist Party was founded here in 1879, just 19 years after the bar was established, and Casa Labra has been producing typically *madrileño* tapas ever since. Tasty cod croquettes are a house specialty.

🞤 F7 ✉ Calle Tetuán 12 ☎ 91 531 00 81 🕓 Restaurant Mon–Sat 1.15–3.30, 8.15–10; bar has longer hours, including Sun 🚇 Sol

CASA REVUELTA (€)

This homey, no-frills bar is famed for its cod fritter (*bacalau*) tapas, which are light, crispy and delicious, especially when washed down with an ice-cold *cerveza*. It's very popular with locals, especially midday on Sundays.

🞤 E8 ✉ Calle de Latoneros 3 ☎ 91 366 33 32 🕓 Tue–Sat 2.30–4, 7–11, Sun 10.30–4 🚇 Sol

CERVECERÍA CERVANTES (€)

This place specializes in seafood, and is always packed with locals Just point at what you fancy. The *tostada de gamba*, hot shrimps in aioli on toast, are quite delicious.

🞤 G8 ✉ Plaza de Jesús 7 ☎ 91 429 60 93 🕓 Daily 11am–midnight 🚇 Antón Martín

CHOCOLATERÍA SAN GINÉS (€)

chocolateriasangines.com

An institution in the city, dating from 1894, this café is famed for its hot chocolate and churros and the fact that it is open 24 hours. It's a favorite stop for the post-partying crowd, particularly on weekends.

🞤 F7 ✉ Pasaje de San Ginés 5 ☎ 91 365 65 46 🕓 Daily 24 hours 🚇 Sol, Ópera

LHARDY (€€–€€€)

lhardy.com

Dating from 1839, this classy restaurant is a local institution. Tapas are served downstairs and, in summer, it has Madrid's best gazpacho. There is also a delicatessen.

F7 ⊠ Calle Carrera de San Jerónimo 8 ☎ 91 521 33 85 🕐 Mon–Sat 1–3.30, 8.30–11, Sun 1–3.30 🚇 Sol

MERCADO DE SAN MIGUEL (€)

A short stroll from Plaza Mayor, one of the city's most beautiful former markets, set in an early 20th-century building, has metamorphosed into a hip eating spot with a diverse range of food counters serving everything from oysters and cava to paella.

E7 ⊠ Plaza San Miguel ☎ 91 542 49 36 🕐 Thu–Sat 10am–2am, Sun–Wed 10am–midnight 🚇 Sol

POSADA DE LA VILLA (€€€)

posadadelavilla.com

The building, just off the Plaza Mayor, dates back to 1642, and the atmosphere and dishes are pure Castilian. This is the place to order Madrid oven-roast lamb and chickpea stew (order 24 hours in advance).

E8 ⊠ Cava Baja 9 ☎ 91 366 18 60 🕐 Mon–Sat 1–4, 8–midnight, Sun 1–4 🚇 Latina, Tirso de Molina, Sol

TABERNA DE ANTONIO SÁNCHEZ (€)

tabernaantoniosanchez.com

The best-conserved of all the tapas bars pays homage to the *madrileño* family that has run it since 1830. Historic photos and memorabilia make the setting as interesting as the tapas.

F8 ⊠ Calle Mesón de Paredes 13 ☎ 91 539 78 26 🕐 Mon–Sat 12–4, 8–midnight, Sun 12–4 🚇 Tirso de Molina

TABERNA MACEIRA (€)

tabernamaceira.com

Join the *madrileños* standing outside and wait for a table in this popular Galician-style haunt. The music is Galician bagpipes and the helpings are large. Try the *pimientos de padrón* (green peppers). It's cramped, noisy and good value. Payment is cash only, and you can't reserve ahead.

G8 ⊠ Calle de las Huertas 66 ☎ 91 429 58 18 🕐 Daily 1–4.30, 10.30–1 🚇 Antón Martín

LA VINOTECA BARBECHERA (€)

vinoteca-barbechera.com

Part of a successful chain of wine bars, this is a good place to see modern Madrid at play. A good range of snacks is offered—platters of smoked tuna and trout, *tostas* (toast) topped with leeks and Brie, apple tart for dessert—plus a wide range of wines by the glass from Spain and abroad. There are six venues in Madrid, including one in Chueca.

G8 ⊠ Calle del Príncipe 27 ☎ 91 420 04 78 🕐 Daily 10am–midnight 🚇 Antón Martín, Sol

VIUDA DE VACAS (€)

viudadevacas.es

Madrileños like to bring their overseas visitors here for traditional Spanish dishes like *rabo de toro* (oxtail), served in a vaulted brick dining room dating from 1887.

E8 ⊠ Calle Cava Alta 23 ☎ 91 366 58 47 🕐 Mon, Wed–Sat 1–4.30, 8–midnight, Sun 1–4.30 🚇 La Latina

---

MADRID GASTRONOMY

Asado means roast, and there's nothing better than roast lamb or kid from a wood-fired oven. The other major local favorite is *cocido*, a stew with meat, chickpeas and vegetables. These are cooked together in a clay pot, right in the fireplace. Match these with the regional red wines made from Tempranillo grapes.

Home to one of the world's most famous art museums and one of the world's great urban parks, this part of Madrid is a magnet for visitors. Don't miss the Real Fábrica de Tapices, the tapestry factory, where tradition rules.

Jerónimos and the East

5

6

7

8

9

SERRANO

VELAZQUEZ

Calle

de

Serrano

Mercado

RECOLETOS

Plaza
de Colón

Centro Cultural
Villa de Madrid

CALLE

DE

DI

Jardines del
Descubrimiento

DE

Lagasca

Biblioteca
Nacional

Calle

Coello

de

Jorge

CALLE

Jua

Museo
Arqueológico
Nacional

de

RECOLETOS

Claudio

de

Villanueva

ESTACIÓN
DE RECOLETOS

Calle

CALLE

Calle del Conde Aranda

DE

Palacio Marquis
de Salamanca

Retiro

San Manuel y
San Benito

DE

PASEO

Casa de
América

Plaza de la
Independencia

CALLE

Puerta
de Alcalá

Puerta
Hernani

P
Ga

Plaza de
la Cibeles

Puerta
Independencia

Plaza
Maestro
Villa

Palacio
de Cibeles

Avenida Méjico

Plaza
Nicaragua

Paseo

Calle de Montalbán

Museo
Naval

Museo Artes
Decorativas

Paseo de la Argentina

Alfonso
XII

PASEO DEL PRADO

PASEO DEL PRADO

Calle Juan de Mena

Puerta
España

Bolsa
de Madrid

Calle de Antonio Maura

CALLE

Plaza de
la Lealtad

Casón del
Buen Retiro

Plaza de
Honduras

Plaza
Canovas
del Castillo

Calle de Felipe IV

Museo del
Prado

Calle de la Academia

San Jerónimo
el Real

DE

Puerta
Murillo

Paseo de Marqués de Pontejos

ALFONSO

JERÓNIMOS

Calle

de

Moreto

PASEO

Plaza
de
Murillo

Calle

de

Espalter

Paseo de la Chopera

DEL

Real Jardin
Botánico

XII

PRADO

Puerta
del Angel
Caido

Paseo del Duque de Fernán Núñez

Calle Claudio Moyano

Viveros
Municipal

Plaza del
Emperador
Carlos V

Ministerio de Agricultura y Pesca,
Alimentación y Medio Ambiente

Museo Nacional
de Antropología

Observatorio
Astronómico

Calle

de

PASE

AVENIDA DE LA CIUDAD DE BARCELONA

Atocha
Renfe

Panteón
Hombres
Ilustres

Estación
de Atocha

Basilica
Señora de
Atocha

0   250 m

0   250 yds

G

H

de Ayala

SALAMANCA

Hermosilla

Velázquez

CALLE PRÍNCIPE DE VERGARA

Calle del General Pardiñas

GOYA

La Concepción

Calle de Castelló

Príncipe de
Vergara

Acuña

ALCALÁ

Puerta de
Madrid

Plaza
Costa Rica

Glorieta
Sevilla

Calle Antonio

AVENIDA

via

Paseo del Duque de Fernán Núñez

olombia

DE

Plaza de
Guatemala

MENÉNDEZ

Glorieta
Sardana

Paseo de Venezuela

Paseo del Duque de Fernán Núñez

Jardines del
Arquit Herrero
Palacios

Y

Palacio de
Velázquez

PELAYO

alacio
Cristal

Jardines
de Cecilio
Rodríguez

**Parque
del Retiro**

Puerta
Granada

Paseo de Uruguay

Puerta del
Pacífico

orieta
Ángel
aldo

La
Rosaleda

Paseo del Duque de Fernán Núñez

Calle Poeta Esteban Villegas

DE MENÉNDEZ Y PELAYO

lle Andrés

Plaza
Mariano
de Cavia

EINA CRISTINA

Calle de
Gutenberg

AVENIDA

Torreton

**Real Fábrica
de Tapices**

J   K   L

Museo Arqueológico Nacional

TOP 25

Roman sculptures in the sou courtyard (below); the Dam Oferente, a second-century Iberian statue (right)

Now thoroughly modernized, Madrid's Archaeological Museum displays its fascinating collection of finds, from prehistory to modern times, around two naturally lit courtyards.

What has changed What was once a confusing, rather stuffy museum has metamorphosed into an exciting modern display of priceless antiquities set in 40 light and airy exhibition spaces that combine glass, stone and wood. Everything is well labeled in Spanish and English, while audiovisual displays, maps and graphic panels help to place the pieces in their historical context. A contemporary café is another welcome addition.

The collection The museum's vast collection totals some 13,000 objects, which trace human evolution from prehistoric times, with artifacts from Greek, Egyptian, Roman, Paleochristian, Visigothic and Muslim cultures. Particularly fascinating is the fact that the majority of pieces displayed were discovered during excavations in Spain, reflecting the wealth and diversity of the human settlements here. There is plenty to stimulate children, including a room that houses the remains of a 3.2-million-year-old female, affectionately known as Lucy, which includes videos that show what life was like during the period when she lived. There is also a reconstruction of Spain's famous Altamira caves and their prehistoric paintings of horses, deer, bison and animal-headed humans.

THE BASICS

man.es
+ H6
✉ Calle de Serrano 13
☎ 91 577 79 12
🕐 Tue–Sat 9.30–8, Sun 9.30–3
🍽 Café with outside terrace
Ⓢ Serrano
🚃 Recoletos
🚌 5, 14, 27, 45, 150
♿ Good
💷 Inexpensive; free Sat after 2 and Sun

HIGHLIGHTS

● La Dama de Baza
● La Dama de Elche (the Spanish "Mona Lisa")
● Mummies
● Reproduction of Altamira cave paintings
● Visigoth crown

TIP

● Note that if you want to rent an audio guide you will need to show ID

Museo del Prado

The city's pride in the magnificent Prado is justified. With its Goyas, El Grecos and other masterpieces, it is undoubtedly one of the great art museums of the world.

Brief history The neoclassical building, completed by Juan de Villanueva in 1785, was conceived by Carlos III as a center for the study of natural sciences. After Napoléon's troops damaged it during the Spanish Wars of Succession, it was restored by Fernando VII as a home for the royal collection of paintings and sculptures and opened as a museum in November 1819. The collection numbers 7,000 pictures, of which around 1,500 are on display at any given time; there are 115 Goyas, 83 works by Rubens, 50 by Velázquez, 40 Brueghels, 36 Titians, 32 El Grecos and

20 Zurbaráns. The new wing is used for temporary exhibitions, often of masterpieces that have been kept in storage due to lack of wall space in the main galleries.

Velázquez and Goya Do not leave the Prado without seeing Velázquez's masterpiece, *Las Meninas* (*The Ladies-in-Waiting*, 1656), widely considered technically the finest painting in the world. Goya's *Majas*—two paintings believed to be of the Duchess of Alba, one naked, one clothed—positively beckon the spectator into the picture, Madrid's seductive answer to the *Mona Lisa*. Goya's *Pinturas negras* (Black Paintings)—among them *Saturn Devouring One of his Sons* and *Half-Drowned Dog*—reflect his dark outlook on the world in his later life and are at once grotesque and breathtaking.

THE BASICS

museoprado.es

✚ H8

✉ Paseo del Prado

🕐 Mon–Sat 10–8, Sun 10–7

☎ 91 330 28 00

🍴 Restaurant, café

🚇 Atocha, Recoletos

🚊 Banco de España, Atocha

🚌 9, 10, 14, 19, 27, 34, 37, 45

♿ Good

💶 Expensive. Under-18s and students free. Also free Mon–Sat 6–8pm, Sun 5–7pm

Monument to Alfonso XII (opposite and right); fun in the park (below)

Parque del Retiro

Small enough to be welcoming, but large enough to get pleasantly lost in, the Retiro will linger in your memory, particularly if you see it in late spring or early autumn, when its colors are most vivid.

History On a sunny Sunday afternoon, the whole city seems drawn to the Retiro park, 1.2sq km (0.5sq miles) in the city center, whose name translates as "retreat". Originally thickly wooded and once a hunting ground for Felipe II, the Retiro was the brainchild of the Duke of Olivares, who designed it in the 1630s for Felipe IV as part of the Buen Retiro Palace—a complex of royal buildings and immense formal gardens that inspired Louis XIV at Versailles. It was used until the time of Carlos III, who opened part of it to the public in the 1770s. Most of the palace was destroyed during the Napoleonic Wars.

A walk in the park Use the entrance on Calle Alfonso XII, opposite the Casón del Buen Retiro. Walk through the parterre gardens and up the steps along a broad, shady avenue to the lake. If you want to take a boat out, head left around the lake; otherwise, turn right and follow the Paseo de Republica de Cuba. From here, you can take one of many paths leading to the Palacio de Cristál (Glass Palace), the Retiro's loveliest building. Built in 1886, it is one of several exhibition spaces in the park. At the southern end of the park is La Rosaleda (the Rose Garden), in its fullest glory in May.

THE BASICS

✚ H7–J8

✉ Calle Alcalá, Alfonso XII, Avenida de Menedez Pelayo, Paseo de la Reina Cristina

🕐 May–Sep 6am–midnight; Oct–Apr 6am–10pm

🍴 Terrazas

🚉 Atocha, Retiro

Ⓜ Retiro, Atocha, Ibiza

🚌 2, 19, 20, 26, 28, 52, 148

HIGHLIGHTS

● Palacio de Cristál
● Horse-drawn carriage tours of the park
● Cecilio Rodríguez Gardens
● Velázquez Palace
● Statue of Alfonso XII
● Lake
● Fallen Angel statue
● 400-year-old cypress tree near Philip IV entrance
● Philip IV parterre
● Observatory (1790)
● Free band concerts from May to October
● Puppet shows for children on Sunday

Plaza de la Cibeles

HIGHLIGHTS

● Post Office
● Gardens of Palacio de Linares
● Facade of Bank of Spain building
● Robert Michel's lions
● Newspaper stand on Paseo del Prado

This is one of the grandest plazas in the city, centered on a statue of a goddess on a chariot drawn by lions, which, to *madrileños*, is as much a symbol of the city as the Colosseum is to Romans.

Cars pass by Seated imperiously at one of Madrid's busiest intersections, the goddess and her marble fountain were erected according to instructions from Carlos III (1716–88). The main statue is by Francisco Gutiérrez and the lions, Hipponomes and Atlanta, drawing the goddess's chariot, are by Robert Michel. Originally at the corner of the square, the statue was finally completed in 1792 and moved in 1895, at which date the cherubim were added. Fans of Real Madrid have unofficially adopted the statue and gather here to celebrate wins.

Clockwise from left: The fountain of La Cibeles, named after Cybele, Phrygian goddess or agriculture and fertility, stands in the middle of the square; the goddess holds a scepter and a key atop her chariot; opulent limestone facade of the Palacio Linares

Around the plaza The enormous wedding-cake look-alike on the southeastern side of the square is one of Madrid's most imposing buildings. Its painstakingly worked facade reminiscent of Viennese style, it was designed in 1904 to be the Palacio de Comunicaciones (Post Office), but was dubbed by local wits as Our Lady of Communications, as if it were a cathedral. The building is now used by the Madrid City Council.

The Palacio de Linares The real treasure of the Plaza de la Cibeles is the elaborate Palacio de Linares. It was designed in 1872 for the noble Linares family and sumptuously decorated. Restored and opened in 1992 as the Casa de América, it now showcases exhibits about Latin American visual arts.

THE BASICS

- ✚ H7
- ✉ Plaza de la Cibeles
- 🚇 Atocha, Recoletos
- 🚇 Banco de España
- 🚌 5, 9, 10, 14, 20, 27, 34, 45, 51, 53 and all night buses

More to See

CASÓN DEL BUEN RETIRO

museoprado.es

This was originally the ballroom of the Buen Retiro Royal Palace, a building destroyed by Napoleonic troops but rebuilt by Carlos III, who had the vault decorated with frescoes. It holds free exhibitions.

🔢 H8 ✉ Calle Alfonso XII 68 ☎ 902 10 70 77 🚇 Retiro, Banco de España 🚌 9, 10, 14, 27, 37, 45 ♿ Few

ESTACIÓN DE ATOCHA

A vast indoor tropical garden can be found inside this late 19th-century wrought-iron station canopy by Alberto del Palacio. The cylindrical glass tower nearby is a monument to the 191 victims of the 2004 bomb attacks on Madrid trains.

🔢 H9 ✉ Plaza del Emperador Carlos V ☎ 90 210 00 07 🚇 Atocha 🚌 14, 27, 34, 37, 45 ♿ Few

JARDINES DEL DESCUBRIMIENTO

Typical of Madrid circa 1970s, these sculpture gardens in the Plaza de Colón were built to celebrate Spain's role in the discovery of the New World. There is an 1892 Jerónimo Suñol statue of Christopher Columbus, but the real highlight here are the Joaquín Vaquero Turcios sculptures. Beneath the gardens is the Centro Cultural de la Villa de Madrid.

🔢 H6 ✉ Plaza de Colón 🚇 Recoletos 🚇 Serrano 🚌 1, 5, 9, 14, 19, 21, 27, 37, 45, 51, 53, 74, 89

PLAZA DE LA LEALTAD

A stone's throw from the Prado, this elegant, semicircular plaza dominated by the Ritz Hotel has an obelisk in the middle to the memory of those who died at the hands of Napoleonic troops on 3 May 1808. Their ashes are kept in an urn at the base of the monument. The Madrid Stock Exchange was built here in 1884, in a neoclassical design that neatly echoes the Prado.

🔢 H7 ✉ Plaza de la Lealtad 🚇 Banco de España 🚌 10, 14, 27, 34, 37, 45

Estación de Atocha

Casón del Buen Retiro

PUERTO DE ALCALÁ

Listed as a National Monument, this gateway in the Plaza de la Independencia was commissioned by Carlos III in 1778 and is perhaps the city's finest example of neoclassical architecture. Come to see it floodlit at night.

🔲 H7 ✉ Plaza de la Independencia 🚇 Recoletos 🚇 Retiro 🚌 9, 15, 20, 28, 51, 52

REAL FÁBRICA DE TAPICES

realfabricadetapices.com

The looms still hum in the Royal Tapestry Factory as they did in the 18th century, when the Flemish van der Goten family founded the works. On the tour (40 minutes), you learn that many of the original designs were created by Goya and other famous artists, and that it can take four months to finish one square meter.

🔲 J9 ✉ Calle de Fuenterrabía 2 ☎ 91 434 05 50 🕐 Mon–Fri 10–2. Closed Aug 🚇 Atocha, Menéndez Pelayo 🚌 14, 24, 26, 32, 37, 54, 141 ♿ None 💶 Inexpensive

REAL JARDÍN BOTÁNICO

rjb.csic.es

These peaceful gardens are the result of overseas expeditions in search of interesting species dating back to the 18th century. The plants and trees are carefully classified and laid out along geometrical walkways. It's the perfect retreat from the city.

🔲 H8 ✉ Plaza de Murillo 2 🕐 Daily from 10am; closing varies with season 🚇 Atocha 🚌 10, 14, 27, 34, 37, 45 💶 Inexpensive

SAN JERÓNIMO EL REAL

Iglesia de San Jerónimo el Real, Madrid's society church, wedged at the side of the Prado, was built in 1505, but over the centuries renovations included controversial neo-Gothic additions. The steps at the entrance on Calle Alarcón, for example, were built for the wedding of Alfonso XIII and his queen, Victoria Eugenia, in 1906.

🔲 H8 ✉ Calle Moreto 4 ☎ 91 420 35 78 🕐 Daily 10–1, 5–8 🚇 Atocha, Banco de España ♿ Difficult 💶 Free

Craftspeople at work at the Royal Tapestry Factory

Shopping

CUESTA MOYANO

Located close to El Retiro park, this row of small kiosks specialize in selling books and postcards, but also carry some quirkier souvenir-style items such as historic black-and-white posters of Madrid and similar.

🔲 H9 ✉ Cuesta Moyano 🚇 Atocha

IMAGINARIUM

imaginarium.es

Much more than a children's toy shop, this is all about what the name promises: imagination. From musical toys to dolls, the idea is to encourage children to have fun, in a creative, yet educational way.

🔲 H9 ✉ Plaza del Emperador Carlos V ☎ 91 506 21 23 🚇 Atocha

EL JARDÍN DE SERRANO

jardindeserrano.es

This select shopping mall occupies two restored 19th-century mansions on the corner of calles Goya and Serrano. The well-heeled stores inside sell fashion, jewelry, gifts, toys and accessories.

🔲 H6 ✉ Calle de Goya 6–8 ☎ 91 577 00 12 🚇 Serrano

MUSEO DEL PRADO

tiendaprado.com

The museum's excellent shop is a great place to find quality souvenirs. As well as reproductions of famous works, there are silk scarves and blouses, pictures and chocolates, ties and jewelry.

🔲 H8 ✉ Paseo del Prado ☎ 91 330 28 00 🚇 Banco de España

NATURA

naturaselection.es

Dedicated to arts and crafts, plus clothes from South America, Asia and Africa, this store sells one-of-a-kind items, with scarves and bags, lamps and gloves—all made of natural materials.

🔲 H9 ✉ Plaza del Emperador Carlos V ☎ 91 467 21 28 🚇 Atocha

OBJETOS DE ARTE TOLEDANO

armasmedievales.com

This unusual shop specializes in medieval-style swords, shields and clothing, as well as antique weaponry. Many of the swords are made in nearby Toledo and are truly beautiful works of art.

🔲 G8 ✉ Paseo del Prado 10 ☎ 91 429 50 00 🚇 Atocha

PERFUMERÍA ALVAREZ GOMEZ

alvarezgomez.com

There are branches of this long-established perfumery all over Madrid. They sell a huge range of cosmetics and scents, but mostly their own delicate, flowery fragrances and colognes, beautifully bottled and excellent value.

🔲 H6 ✉ Calle de Serrano 14 ☎ 91 431 16 56 🚇 Retiro

PIEL DE TORO

pieldetoro.com

This traditional Madrid shop is famed for its T-shirts, sweatshirts and baseball caps bearing their distinctive bull emblem.

🔲 H8 ✉ Paseo del Prado 42 ☎ 91 360 07 52 🚇 Atocha

ANTIQUES

Madrid's amazing array of antiques shops are in three main areas: the *barrio* Salamanca, around the Calle del Prado and Santa Ana, and around the Rastro, particularly down the Calle Ribera de Curtidores—the most likely source for bargains. Many shops do not specialize in any particular goods, but sell a broad selection of merchandise.

JERÓNIMOS AND THE EAST SHOPPING

Entertainment and Nightlife

DISCOTECA AZÚCAR

azucarsalsadisco.com

Even if you can't salsa, you can have lessons every night at this popular Latin American club where the music is persistent and the crowd is full of fun.

➕ J9 ✉ Calle Atocha 107 ☎ 91 402 16 40 ⏰ Thu 10pm–5am, Fri–Sat 11.30pm–6am 🚇 Atocha

FLORIDA PARK

floridaretiro.com

Located within Retiro Park, Florida Park has long been a popular destination for out-of-town visitors who enjoy a show and dancing late into the night. It has a restaurant, dance floor and stage.

➕ J7 ✉ Avenida de Menéndez Pelayo (al Ibiza) ☎ 91 573 78 04 ⏰ Tue–Sat 9pm–3am 🚇 Ibiza

EL RETIRO

Sundays in the park (▷ 75) are famous for the many entertainers and musicians who keep old and young amused. Outstanding are the summer concerts, called *Veranos de la Villa*.

TEATRO KAPITAL

grupo-kapital.com

The seven dance floors here offer everything from salsa to karaoke and R'n'B, and there's a cinema. The great attraction in summer is the rooftop terrace. Teenagers dominate in the early evening, with grown-ups flooding in later, when the dress code is smart-casual.

➕ H9 ✉ Calle de Atocha 125 ☎ 91 420 29 06 ⏰ Fri–Sat 5.30pm–10.30pm, Thu–Sun midnight–6am 🚇 Atocha

---

MADRID BY NIGHT

Main bar areas in the center of the city are the start of the Paseo de la Castellana (sophisticated), Malasaña (thoroughly unsophisticated), La Latina and Santa Ana, and Chueca.

Where to Eat

PRICES

Prices are approximate, based on a 3-course meal for one person.

€€€	over €60
€€	€35–€60
€	under €35

ÁLBORA (€€€)

restaurantealbora.com

Star chef Raul Prior's restaurant is geared to leading-edge fashion food. Every dish—from salads, carpaccios and the finest Spanish hams to pastas and desserts—is a treat for the eye. There's also a bar with longer opening hours serving simpler dishes and tapas.

➕ J6 ✉ Calle de Jorge Juan 33 ☎ 91 781 61 97 ⏰ Mon–Sat 1.30–4, 8.30–11.30 🚇 Velázquez, Retiro

EL BOTÁNICO (€€€)

restaurantebotanico.com

A block from the Prado, this peaceful bar-restaurant has a shady terrace and spacious interior. The menu offers solid Spanish specialties, such as excellent paella, as well as pasta and salad.

🔲 H7 ✉ Calle Ruiz de Alarcón 27 ☎ 91 420 23 42 🕐 Daily 8am–2am; food served till 11pm 🚇 Banco de España

LA CASTELA (€€)

lacastela.com

A local favorite, this sophisticated spot is part tapas bar and part dining room specializing in Spanish cuisine, such as oxtail, and seafood. Reserve ahead.

🔲 K7 ✉ Calle del Doctor Castelo 22 ☎ 91 573 55 90 🕐 Mon–Sat 2–4, 9–midnight 🚇 Ibiza, Príncipe de Vergara

LA GAMELLA (€€€)

lagamella.com

In a splendid old building that was the birthplace of Spanish philosopher José Ortega y Gasset, this small American-owned restaurant offers contemporary fusion cooking combining Spanish and American influences: steak tartare with a shot of Jack Daniels, a classic Caesar salad and proper burgers.

🔲 H7 ✉ Calle de Alfonso XII 4 ☎ 91 532 45 09 🕐 Mon–Thu 1.30–4, 9–11.30, Fri–Sat 1.30–4, 9–12.30 🚇 Retiro

LA HOJA (€€)

lahoja.es

Free-range chicken and organic vegetables form the base of much of the cooking at this straightforward, but elegant family-run restaurant, where the emphasis is on Asturian-style recipes.

🔲 K7 ✉ Calle del Doctor Castelo 48 ☎ 91 409 25 22 🕐 Tue–Thu noon–midnight, Fri–Sat 8pm–midnight, Sun 12–6 🚇 Ibiza, Príncipe de Vergara

LA MONTERÍA (€€)

lamonteria.es

This tastefully revamped restaurant and tapas bar is always busy with a loyal local clientele. One of the specialties

here is *salmoreja* (a thick, garlicky version of gazpacho). Or try the lightly battered shrimp or the artichoke and asparagus risotto.

🔲 K7 ✉ Calle Lope de Rueda 25 ☎ 91 574 18 12 🕐 Mon–Sat 2–4, 8.30–11 🚇 Príncipe de Vergara

RESTAURANTE VIRIDIANA (€€€)

restauranteviridiana.com

At one of Madrid's finest restaurants, expect complex modern dishes using traditional and high-quality Spanish produce. The wine list is one of the best in the city.

🔲 H7 ✉ Calle de Juan de Mena 14 ☎ 91 531 10 39 🕐 Daily 1.30–4, 8.30–midnight 🚇 Banco de España, Retiro

TRATTORIA SANT'ARCANGELO (€€)

trattoriasantarcangelo.es

Just a few steps from the Prado and the Jardín Botánico, this is one of Madrid's best contemporary Italian restaurants. Top dishes include crispy pizzas, spaghetti with seafood sauce and tiramisu.

🔲 H8 ✉ Calle de Moreto 15 ☎ 91 369 10 93 🕐 Daily 12–4, 8–11 🚇 Banco de España

TAPAS

Tapas, snacks to accompany your drink, are a part of Spanish culture. They started in the 18th century when Carlos III insisted that his entourage cover their wine with a plate of food to keep dust from getting into it (*tapa* means "lid"). Many bars no longer display their wares, which can make it hard to order; it's easier when the tapas are kept behind glass so you can see them before buying. Pay before leaving, rather than on a round-by-round basis. Many *cervecerías* (late-night bars) sell tapas and make an atmospheric venue for a night-time snack.

The heart of the city's gay scene, Chueca is a vibrant, fashionable *barrio* that is home to some of the best cafés, nightlife and shopping in Madrid, while neighboring Malasaña still reflects the spirit of the *movida* that flourished here in the 1980s.

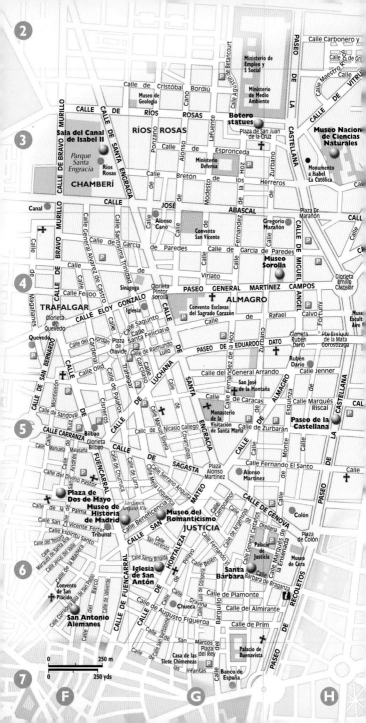

Map labels

Plaza de la República Argentina

AVENIDA DEL DOCTOR ARCE

EL VISO

Calle de Rodríguez Marín

Calle Emilio

Calle Callarza

Calle Marqués de Villamagna

de Valderiban

Calle Loriga

Calle Felipe IV

Auditorio Nacional de Música

Calle de Suero de Quiñones

Prosperidad

Calle de Cartagena

CALLE DE JOAQUÍN COSTA

VELAZQUEZ de

Calle A Rodríguez Villa

Calle Gabriel Lobo

Calle Campos

Cruz del Rayo

Calle de Cartagena

General

Cabrera

Zabala

SERRANO

Manrique

Calle

DE

Calle de

Calle Ortega de Sevilla

Calle Antonio Pérez

CALLE

PRÍNCIPE

DE

VERGARA

Calle de Luis de

Calle de Canillas

Quintiliano

CALLE DE CARTAGENA

Calle Pablo Aranda

Calle de San Julio

Miguel de los Santos

Calle Pinilla del Valle

Calle Castillón de la Plata

Glorieta López de Hoyos

Calle de San Fernando de Jarama

Pedro de

Valdivia

HOYOS

CALLE

Avenida de América

Avenida de América

AVENIDA DE AMÉRICA

LÓPEZ

DE

MOLINA

VERGARA

DE FRANCISCO SILVELA

Gimnasio Moscardó

Calle de Coslada

Museo Lázaro Galdiano

Coello

Lagasca

del

VELAZQUEZ

Balboa

General

Castelló

Santa Mónica

Oráa

Pardiñas

Porlier

Convento P. Dominicos

CALLE

Núñez

DE

de

DIEGO

San Francisco de Borja

La Virgen Peregrino

DE

LEÓN

Diego de León

General

Díaz

Núñez de Balboa

Maldonado

PRÍNCIPE

Calle

del

General

Maldonado

CALLE

DE

JUAN

BRAVO

de

Calle

Nuestra Señora del Pilar

ASTELLANA

Calle

San Andrés Flamencos

CALLE

DE

Padilla

Castelló

Calle

del

Calle

de

Fundación Juan March

JOSÉ ORTEGA Y GASSET

Plaza Marqués de Salamanca

Coello

Lagasca

de

Don Ramón

Cruz

Núñez de Balboa

Rosario

Claudio

Santa María de Monte Carmelo

Calle

de

la

Cruz

Ayala

Calle

de

Ayala

J K

Museo Lázaro Galdiano

HIGHLIGHTS

● *Landscape* by Gainsborough
● *St. John in Patmos* by Bosch
● *Luis de Góngora* by Velázquez
● *The Adoration of the Magi* by El Greco

TIP

● Take one of the free guided tours on Sat or Sun at 11.30am.

This museum, set in an imposing 20th-century mansion, is home to a wonderfully ecelctic collection of some 13,000 paintings and art objects—so there is always something new to discover.

A noble art collector José Lázaro Galdiano was born into Navarre nobility and became an obsessive, seemingly unfocused art collector, who died in 1947 at the age of 85. He married Paola Florido, an Argentinian who shared his love for art, and together they devoted their lives to traveling the world in search of treasures. An essentially private man, Lázaro never revealed how much he paid for any of the masterpieces. On his death, he donated his collection to the state, and the museum opened in 1951. The exhibition begins on the

From left: Portrait of a Lady *by Thomas Gainsborough;* The Crusaders before Jerusalem *by Eugenio Lucas Velázquez (1817–1870)*

ground floor with an assessment of Lázaro's role as patron and collector and displays a sample of the collection, which includes paintings by Hieronymus Bosch, Bartolomé Murillo, Rembrandt, Francisco Zurbarán, El Greco, Velázquez, José de Ribera, Turner and Goya, as well as exquisite gold and silverwork, bronzes, stained glass, jewelry, fans and weaponry.

Parque Florido The collection is housed in the Parque Florido, a neo-Renaissance palazzo named after Lázaro's wife. The beautifully restored interiors provide a magnificent setting for the treasures on display. Don't miss the spectacular painted ceilings, commissioned by Lázaro to decorate what were originally the family's private apartments. This is the finest of Madrid's smaller art galleries.

THE BASICS

flg.es

➕ J4

✉ Serrano 122

☎ 91 561 60 84

🕐 Tue–Sat 10–4.30, Sun 10–3

🚇 Nuñez de Balboa/ Rubén Dario, Gregorio Marañón

🚌 9, 12, 16, 19, 51

♿ Good

💰 Moderate. Reduced price for over-60s and students. First Fri of month free 5–9pm

Museo Sorolla

HIGHLIGHTS

● *La Bata Rosa* (Room II)
● *Self Portrait* (Room III)
● *Clotilde en traje de noche* (Room III)
● *Clotilde en traje gris* (Room III)
● Turkish bed (Room III)
● *La Siesta* (Room IV)
● *Las Velas* (Room IV)
● *Nadadores* (Room V)
● *Madre* (Room VI)
● New York gouaches (Drawings Room)

TIP

● The lovely gardens here are a great spot to head to for some peace and quiet in bustling Madrid.

This serene spot belonged to Spain's finest Impressionist, Valencian Joaquín Sorolla, who wanted to create an oasis of peace for himself in a busy city. It is the best of Madrid's house museums.

Entrance and gardens The Sorolla Museum is one of the few places in the city to give us a sense of the shape of an artist's life and work. Built in 1910–11 by Enrique María de Repollés, it was the Madrid home of Joaquín Sorolla (1863–1923) and became a museum after Sorolla's widow, Clotilde, donated it to the state. The two small gardens, designed by Sorolla himself as a setting for his collection of fountains and fonts, are a bit of Andalucía in Madrid. The first is an imitation of a part of the Seville *alcázar*, while the second is modeled on the

Statues in the beautiful gardens of Museo Sorolla (left and right)

Generalife Gardens in Granada's Alhambra. Near the entrance is a replica of a white marble bust of Sorolla by Mariano Benlliure, and to the left is an Andalucian patio.

Inside Lovingly preserved, the house is filled with turn-of-the-20th-century elegance. The ground floor, with its salon and dining room, gives a real feeling of the artist's life and displays his collection of antique pottery. The upper floor has been converted into a gallery, each room given over to a different aspect of Sorolla's work. Be sure to visit his studio, complete with a Turkish bed for the afternoon siesta. Sorolla is famed for his spectacular use of light—check out, for example, *Paseo a Orillas del Mar* (1909), of his wife and daughter walking along a sunlit beach.

THE BASICS

museosorolla.mcu.es

✚ H4

✉ Paseo del General Martínez Campos 37

☎ 91 310 15 84

🕐 Tue–Sat 9.30–8, Sun 10–3

Ⓜ Iglesia, Rubén Darío, Gregorio Marañón

🚌 5, 14, 16, 27, 45, 61, 147, 150

♿ Few

💷 Inexpensive. Free to under-18s, EU citizens over 65, Sun

More to See

BOTERO STATUES

In 1994, a section of Castellana was devoted to an exhibition of sculptures by 20th-century sculptor Fernando Botero. When the exhibition ended, *madrileños* retained a *Hand* in the middle of Castellana; the *Reclining Woman* in Calle Génova; and *Man on a Mule* in the Plaza de Colón.

➕ G/H3 ✉ Plaza de San Juan de la Cruz 🚇 Colón, Nuevos Ministerios 🚌 7, 14, 27, 40, 147, 150

FUNDACIÓN JUAN MARCH

march.es

One of Europe's most important private art foundations, this is home to some 30 wonderfully diverse annual exhibitions, ranging from the Arts and Crafts Movement to Spanish contemporary art.

➕ J5 ✉ Calle Castelló 77/Calle Padilla 36 ☎ 91 435 42 40 🕐 Mon–Sat 11–8, Sun 10–2. Closed Aug and between exhibitions. Free guided tours during exhibitions, telephone for details 🚇 Nuñez de Balboa 🚌 29, 52 ♿ Very good 🎟 Free

IGLESIA DE SAN ANTÓN

Designed by Pedro Ribera and built by Juan de Villanueva, this example of baroque architecture houses a magnificent art collection, including Goya's *The Last Communion of Saint José de Calasanz*, painted between 1775 and 1780, and architect Ventura Rodríguez's *Dolphins* statue.

➕ G6 ✉ Hortaleza 63 ☎ 91 521 74 73 🚇 Tribunal, Chueca

MUSEO DE HISTORIA DE MADRID

madrid.es/museohistoria

Reopened in 2014 after extensive renovation, this fine museum is housed in a sumptuous pink historical building, complete with an extravagant baroque doorway. The exhibits trace the history of Madrid via all manner of artworks, now displayed in spacious wood-paneled rooms. Don't miss the exquisite 3D model of the city dating from 1830, or Goya's *Allegory of Madrid* in the War of Independence room.

Hand *sculpture in the middle of Paseo de la Castellana*

F6 ⊠ Calle de Fuencarral 78 ☎ 91
701 18 63 ⏰ Tue–Fri 10–8, Sat–Sun 10–2
🚇 Tribunal 🚌 21, 37 ♿ Very good
💷 Free

MUSEO NACIONAL DE CIENCIAS NATURALES

mncn.csis.es

The Natural History Museum collections encompass every branch of the natural sciences from fossils to birds, mammals and reptiles. Each category is arranged by themes over five floors, and there are hands-on and interactive exhibits, and temporary shows.

H3 ⊠ Calle José Gutiérrez Abascal 2
☎ 91 411 13 28 ⏰ Sep–Jun Tue–Fri, Sat 10–8, Sun 10–5; Jul–Aug Tue–Fri, Sat 10–3, Sun 10–5 🚇 Gregorio Marañón, Nuevos Ministerios, Ríos Rosas 🚌 7, 12, 14, 27, 40, 45, 147, 150 ♿ Moderate ❓ Guided tours can be arranged in advance 💷 Moderate

MUSEO DEL ROMANTICISMO

museoromanticismo.mcu.es

This monument to faded Romantic glory, founded in 1924, is inside a mid-18th-century *madrileño* building that was the home of the traveler-painter the Marqués de Véga-Inclán. Though the content might be too sentimental for some, there are many items of interest, particularly Alenza's miniature *Satires of Romantic Suicide,* Goya's *Saint Gregory the Great*, and fine Isabelline and Imperial furniture.

G6 ⊠ Calle San Mateo 13 ☎ 91 448 10 45/91 448 01 63 ⏰ May–Oct Tue–Sat 9.30–8.30, Sun 10–3; Nov–Apr Tue–Sat 9.30–6.30, Sun 10–3 🚇 Tribunal 🚌 21, 37 ♿ Very good 💷 Inexpensive. Free Sat after 2pm

PASEO DE LA CASTELLANA

Running in an almost straight line from Colón for 6.5km (4 miles) to Plaza de Castilla, the Castellana is one of Madrid's main points of reference and a center of business and nightlife. It splits the city in two, and many major sights are on or around it.

H5 🚇 Colón, Rubén Darío, Nuevos Ministerios, Lima, Cuzco, Plaza de Castilla 🚌 5, 14, 27, 40, 45, 147, 149, 150

Museo del Romanticismo

PLAZA DE DOS DE MAYO

On 2 May 1808, during the French occupation, a young girl, Manuela Malasaña, was shot by French soldiers for smuggling a weapon—actually just a pair of scissors. Earlier in the day, two locals had led an attack on the Monteléon artillery barracks to capture arms. The insurgency was quashed, but sparked a four-year-long struggle for independence. The area is called Malasaña in memory of the heroine, and the dramatic statue here honors the two soldiers who died leading the uprising. Today, the square is lined with small bars and restaurants. The date is commemorated each year with a hugely popular festival of parades.
➕ F5 🚇 Bilbao

SALA DEL CANAL DE ISABEL II

Considered one of Madrid's finest examples of industrial architecture, this display space, built between 1907 and 1911, hosts frequent concerts and excellent exhibitions.
➕ F3 ✉ Calle Santa Engracia 125 ☎ 91 445 10 00 🕐 Tue–Sat 11–2, 5–8.30, Sun 11–2 🚇 Ríos Rosas 🚌 3, 12, 21 149 ♿ Good 🎫 Free

SAN ANTONIO ALEMANES

This tiny church dates from the early 17th century and is worth seeing for its splendid floor-to-ceiling frescoes, the work of Neapolitan master Luca Giordano in the 1690s.
➕ F6 ✉ Corredera de San Pablo 16 🕐 Mon–Sat 10.30–2 🚇 Chueca 🚌 21, 37 🎫 Inexpensive

SANTA BÁRBARA (LAS SALESAS REALES)

Probably the grandest of Madrid's churches, Las Salesas was commissioned by Bárbara de Braganza, the wife of Fernando VI. It has an elaborate facade built in the 1750s and contains Sabatini's tomb of Fernando VI (1713–59).
➕ G6 ✉ Calle del General Castaños 2 ☎ 91 319 48 11 🕐 Daily 5–7pm and for Mass 🚇 Alonso Martínez, Colón

Paseo de la Castellana (▷ 91)

A Walk North from Sol

Backstreets and boulevards, an arts center and the up-and-coming area of Malasaña: all are part of this walk.

DISTANCE: 4.6km (2.8 miles) **ALLOW:** 3 hours

START

PUERTA DEL SOL
⊞ F7 🚇 Sol

1 Leave the Puerta del Sol on the northwest side, on the pedestrianized Calle de Preciados. At the Plaza de Callao, bear left on the Gran Vía and follow it, past office blocks and cinemas, to the Plaza de España.

2 Sit on a bench, enjoy the shade and pay your respects to Cervantes, Don Quixote and Sancho Panza, whose statues are at the far side of the square.

3 Now walk up the hill on the Calle de Princesa, into a more residential area. Cross over to the Plaza de Cristino Martos, walk through this small square and follow Calle de Conde Duque, past the huge Cultural Center that used to be in service as an army barracks.

END

GRAN VÍA
⊞ F7 🚇 Gran Vía

7 Exit the square on Calle de Velarde and walk to Calle de Fuencarral. Follow this past the Museo Municipal, currently under renovation, all the way down to Gran Vía.

6 Turn right on Calle de Ruiz and walk down to the Plaza del Dos de Mayo. All around is the Malasaña area, whose little streets are full of tiny shops, bars and clubs.

5 Turn left on Calle de San Bernardo, walk uphill and cross over at the pedestrian crossing. Follow Calle de Divino Pastor, with its little old-fashioned shops and popular bars.

4 Turn right on Calle de Montserrat, immediately right on Calle de Amaniel and stroll through the Plaza de las Comendadoras. Exit the little square on Calle de Quiñones.

93

Shopping

ABC SERRANO SHOPPING CENTER

abcserrano.com

The tiled exterior of what were the ABC newspaper offices now hides a veritable Aladdin's cave of boutiques. With more than 30 to choose from, this is a place to relax and check out the wine, the high fashion and fun jewelry.

🚇 H4/5 ✉ Calle de Serrano 61/Castellana 34 ☎ 91 577 50 31 🚇 Rubén Dario, Nuñez de Balboa, Serrano

CACAO SAMPAKA

cacaosampaka.com

This could be Madrid's most tempting shop. Sampaka sells chocolate but not just bars. There are books and biscuits, jars and molds, drinking chocolate and decorations. The bar-cum-tasting room serves drinks, pastries and desserts.

🚇 H6 ✉ Calle de Orellana 4 ☎ 91 319 58 40 🚇 Alonso Martínez

HOSS

hossintropia.com

This boutique was founded in San Sebastian in 1994 as a fund-raising venture for the homeless and it now has its own label. The designs are casual but stylish, aimed at young professionals. There's another branch in the Salamanca district (Calle Serrano 16).

🚇 F6/7 ✉ Calle Fuencarral 16 ☎ 91 524 17 28 🚇 Gran Vía

IOLI

ioli.shoes

Leather shoes and bags, silk hats and purses, all in vivid colors, are designed and made by Cynthia Ioli, the Argentine owner of this tiny shop. Women's shoes can be made to measure.

🚇 F6 ✉ Calle del Espiritu Santo 1 ☎ 91 521 00 22 🚇 Tribunal

PURIFICACIÓN GARCÍA

purificaciongarcia.com

The sleek look, one of the trademarks of this distinguished Spanish designer of prêt-à-porter men's and women's clothing, is reflected in the minimalist layout of the store.

🚇 E8 ✉ Calle de Serrano 28 and 92 ☎ 91 435 80 13/576 72 76 🚇 Serrano

RESERVA Y CATA

reservaycata.com

Don't miss this excellent *bodega* (wine store) in a Chueca basement, offering some 600 different wines of mainly Spanish origin. Knowledgable staff are on hand to help you choose the perfect bottle of wine for your occasion.

🚇 G6 ✉ Calle de Conde de Xiquena 13 ☎ 91 319 04 01 🚇 Colón

TIENDA OLIVARERO

pco.es

Olive oil lovers will be in heaven at this wonderful place, which is actually an olive oil producers' cooperative. There is plenty of information about the various grades and what they all mean, as well as tastings, and, naturally enough, bottles to buy.

🚇 G5 ✉ Calle Mejia Lequerica ☎ 91 308 05 05 🚇 Alonso Martínez

MADRID FASHION

Madrid has made great leaps forward in the world of men's and women's fashion. The international success of Adolfo Domínguez has been followed by that of Roberto Verino, and together with the avant-garde designs of Agatha Ruiz de la Prada and Jesús del Pozo, the Spanish designers are proving increasingly popular. Salamanca is the best area to go shopping for these designers.

AREIA COLONIAL CHILL OUT

areiachillout.com

DJs perform here nightly. Relax over cocktails and tasty snacks such as falafels and samosas while listening to the music.

🔲 G6 ⊠ Calle de Hortaleza 92 ☎ 91 310 03 07 🕓 Daily 2pm–3.30am 🚇 Tribunal

BUHO REAL

buhoreal.org

The city's "Royal Owl" is the place to see up-and-coming international acts.

🔲 G6 ⊠ Calle Regueros 5 ☎ 91 308 48 51 🕓 Concerts start at 9.30pm, closing times vary 🚇 Alonso Martinez

CAFÉ MANUELA

Dating from the early 1980s with colorful art noveau decor, this café offers board games, all sorts of coffees and drinks and an all-round convivial atmosphere. There is occasional live entertainment, ranging from poetry reading to live music.

🔲 F6 ⊠ San Vincente Ferrer 29 ☎ 91 531 70 37 🕓 Daily 4pm–2.30pm 🚇 Tribunal

CAFÉ LA PALMA

cafelapalma.com

A cross between a conventional café, a wine bar, a Moroccan tea shop and a club. The music in La Palma is just as eclectic—everything from rock 'n' roll to flamenco and Cuban fusion.

🔲 F6 ⊠ Calle de la Palma 62 ☎ 91 522 50 31 🕓 Daily from 4pm 🚇 Noviciado

CAFÉ DE RUIZ

cafederuiz.com

A relatively peaceful retreat from the night-time mayhem of surrounding Malasaña, the Ruiz retains a late 19th-century feel and serves cocktails as well as coffee and milkshakes.

🔲 F5 ⊠ Calle Ruiz 11 ☎ 91 446 12 32 🚇 Bilbao

DEL DIEGO

deldiego.com

Del Diego's superb design and highly attentive staff have quickly made it one of Madrid's best cocktail bars. This is the place to be and be seen.

🔲 G7 ⊠ Calle de la Reina 12 ☎ 91 523 31 06 🕓 Mon–Sat 7pm–3am 🚇 Gran Vía

FORTUNY

palacetefortuny.com

The former palace's terrace garden is Fortuny's best feature. The club is favored by media celebrities and a strict dress code applies. There is a reputable restaurant.

🔲 H4 ⊠ Calle de Fortuny 34 ☎ 91 319 05 88 🕓 Tue–Sun 1.30pm–5am 🚇 Bilbao

OJALÁ

A typical example of the café clubs in Malasaña, this is fun upstairs (movies projected onto walls) and even more fun downstairs, where sand on the floor re-creates summer beach parties. Drinks and snacks are served all day, and dinner in the evening.

🔲 F6 ⊠ Calle de San Andrés 1 ☎ 91 523 27 47 🕓 11am–midnight, later at weekends 🚇 Noviciado, Tribunal

CHUPITO

Don't be surprised if, at the end of a meal in a restaurant, your waiter offers you a *chupito.* Usually served in a shot glass, a *chupito* is small but strong: *orujo de hierbas* (a yellow or green herb liquor), *ponche caballero* (spiced orange brandy), *pacharán* (sloe gin). This is on the house, helps to digest the meal and sends you on your way in a happy frame of mind.

Where to Eat

PRICES

Prices are approximate, based on a 3-course meal for one person.

€€€   over €60
€€   €35–€60
€   under €35

BAZTÁN (€)

An ideal spot to learn more about Spain's best wines, this is a bar in an old taberna, overlooking the historic Plaza del Dos de Mayo. Tapas and other well-prepared snacks are available.

➕ F5 ▦ Calle de San Andrés 14 ☎ 91 523 25 73 ⏰ Tue–Sun noon–midnight, later at weekends 🚇 Tribunal, Bilbao

EL BIERZO (€)

restauranteelbierzobarbieri.com

Lunch is excellent value at this down-to-earth and typical Madrid restaurant, with two different set menus featuring a choice of five or 10 dishes. There's more in the evenings, with well-sourced, fresh produce simply cooked—the various different tortillas are well worth trying. The home-style desserts are also good.

➕ G6 ▦ Calle Barbieri 16 ☎ 91 531 91 10 ⏰ Mon–Sat 1–4, 9–11.30 🚇 Chueca

DSTAGE (€€€)

dstageconcept.com

More of a gastronomic experience than a restaurant, this modern, open-plan establishment is the brainchild of renowned chef Diego Guerrero. There's no à la carte menu—diners choose one of three tasting menus consisting of between 12 and 17 dishes that fuse Spanish, Mexican and Japanese flavors.

➕ G6 ▦ Calle de Regueros 8 ☎ 91 702 15 86 ⏰ Mon–Fri 1.30–3, 9–10.30 🚇 Alonso Martinez

MERCADO DE SAN ANTÓN (€–€€€)

mercadosananton.com

This covered market draws food fans from far and wide. At street level an array of outlets sell a huge range of impeccably sourced produce, and there's also a supermarket. For a sit-down meal, head for the second floor, with its numerous tapas bars, or the restaurant on the uppermost floor with great rooftop views.

➕ G6 ▦ Calle Augusto Figuero 24 ☎ 91 330 07 30 ⏰ Market: Mon–Sat 10–10; bars: daily 10–midnight 🚇 Chueca

LA SACRISTÍA (€€)

la-sacrista.es

Located in the backstreets, this restaurant is a popular haunt of local actors and directors, and is particularly well-known for its *bacalao* (cod) dishes, cooked in various different styles. It also serves excellent paella, steaks and *gambas* (shrimp) served dramatically flamed in whisky.

➕ G7 ▦ Plaza Vázquez de Mella 1 ☎ 91 522 09 45 ⏰ Mon–Sat 1.30–4, 8.30–midnight, Sun 1.30–4 🚇 Gran Via

APERITIFS

Aperitifs are still popular in Spain. Try *vermut* (vermouth), often served on draft from a barrel in many tapas bars. Particularly popular before lunch, vermouth is made from wine infused with herbs and makes an excellent accompaniment for tapas. Order a *vermut con sifón*, with soda, for a refreshing long drink. Sherry is the other great aperitif: *fino* (pale and dry), *manzanilla* (also dry), *amontillado* (a rich, nutty, mature *fino*), *palo cortado* (a rare sherry, between dry and medium), and *oloroso* (rich, but can be dry or sweet).

The hallowed ground that is Real Madrid football club's Bernabéu Stadium is north of central Madrid. And some of the most historic and beautiful cities in Spain are within an hour or so of the city.

Estación
de Chamartín

PASEO DE LA CASTELLANA

AVENIDA DE LA PAZ

TETUÁN

**Real
Madrid**

CHAMARTIN

**Aquópolis San
Fernando de Henares,**
Parque de el Capriche

AVENIDA DE AMÉRICA

Aeroporto
de Madrid-
Barajas

CHAMBERÍ

A2

M30

**Plaza
de Toros**

M110

PASEO DE LA CASTELLANA

SALAMANCA

*Parque Quinta
Fuente del Berro*

M23

MADRID

*Parque
del
Retiro*

RETIRO

AVENIDA DE LA PAZ

M30

CENTRO

Faunia

A3

AVENIDA DEL
MEDITERRÁNEO

Estación
de Atocha

**Madrid
Río**

ARGANZUELA

M30

*Parque
Cerro
del
Tío Pío*

*Parque
Enrique
Tierno
Galvan*

M203

M30

**PUENTE DE
VALLECAS**

USERA

A4/E05

**Warner Bros
Park**

Estación
Entrevías

Farther Afield

Real Madrid

El Estadio Santiago Bernabéu is Real Madrid's home ground (left); club logo (right)

THE BASICS

realmadrid.com

🚇 H1

✉ Calle Conche Espina 1

☎ Stadium: 91 398 43 70; tickets: 902 31 17 09

🕐 Guided tours in English from Gate 7, Mon–Sat 10–7, Sun, public hols 10.30–6.30. No tours 5 hours before match. Sala de Trofeos Tue–Sun 10.30–7.30; closed 3 hours before match

🍴 Café, restaurants

🚇 Santiago Bernabéu

🚌 14

♿ Good

💰 Tour expensive, trophy room moderate

HIGHLIGHTS

● The massive world-famous stadium

● The Trophy Room, with its World and European silverware

● The new Realcafé Bernabéu, with its views

● Any home match, with passionate fans

● The club shop, with its array of replica shirts

● The stadium tour

Founded in 1902, "Real"—or Royal—rose to become one of the world's most famous football clubs. Its impressive achievements were officially recognized by FIFA, the world governing body, in 1988, when it was awarded the accolade "the best club in the history of football".

El Estadio Santiago Bernabéu Real Madrid have their home in the Santiago Bernabéu stadium. The stadium was inaugurated as the Estadio Chamartín (after the old stadium) in 1947, but the name was changed in 1955 in honor of the club's president. Today it holds more than 80,000 spectators, and held well over 100,000 although before UEFA ruled that all standing places had to be converted to seats.

Museum Even if you can't get to a game, you can take a guided tour of the stadium. You will get to enjoy a panoramic view of the inside of the stadium, the pitch and players' tunnel, the away dressing room and the Trophy Room. Unsurprisingly, given the club's illustrious history, this is packed with silver trophies. Numerous video screens show clips from great matches of the past, including *los blancos'* record 12 European Cup triumphs since 1956, as well as 19 Spanish cups and 33 Spanish League championships. Success is not limited to football: Real participates in many sports, notably basketball. Note that tickets for games can be hard to get and should be booked as far in advance as possible.

More to See

AQUÓPOLIS

aquopolis.es

Spanish children beg their parents to take them to Aquópolis, the biggest and best of the Madrid water parks and one of the largest in Europe. There are huge water slides, an adventure lake, a tropical beach and wave machines. There is another Aquópolis at San Fernando de Henares, 15km (9 miles) east of Madrid.

🔲 See map ▷ 98 ✉ Villanueva de la Cañada. Carretera de El Escorial km25 ☎ 902 34 50 06 🕐 Jun, Sep 12–7; Jul–Aug 12–8 🍴 Cafés 💰 Expensive

FAUNIA

faunia.es

This is Europe's only theme park dedicated to nature and biodiversity. The eight pavilions, each of which re-creates a different ecosystem with the authentic sights, sounds, smells, flora and fauna, will amaze and delight. Experience a tropical rainstorm and find out what it's like to live in the Arctic.

🔲 See map ▷ 99 ✉ Avenida de las Comunidades 28 ☎ 91 301 62 35 🕐 Daily from 10am; hours vary 🍴 Cafés 🚇 Valdebernardo 💰 Expensive

MADRID RÍO

This riverside park is a family favorite, with wildlife including ducks and egrets, wonderful views of the Royal Palace, a cycle path and several playgrounds, including one with water jets. There are also several bars and restaurants.

🔲 See map ▷ 99 ✉ Parallel to Rio Manzanares 🚇 Príncipe Pío 🚌 3, 40, 47, 150

PALACIO REAL DE EL PARDO

patrimonionacional.es

Set in a vast park northwest of the city, this former royal palace is usually referred to as El Pardo, after the hill where it stands. Originally a hunting lodge back in 1405, the palace was built for Carlos I and expanded in the 18th century. It was home to General Franco for 35 years. Today, you can visit rooms

Water-park fun

FARTHER AFIELD MORE TO SEE

decorated with fine tapestries designed by Goya and woven at the Real Fábrica de Tapices (▷ 79), as well as murals by Maella and Bayeu.

🗺 See map ▷ 98 ✉ Calle Manuel Alonso, El Pardo ☎ 91 376 15 00 🕐 Apr–Sep daily 10–8; Oct–Mar daily 10–6 🚌 Linea Interurbana 601. By car 14km (8.5 miles) from central Madrid via the M-30, M-605 ♿ Few 💶 Expensive. Free Apr–Sep Wed, Thu 5–8pm; Oct–Mar Wed, Thu 3–6pm

PARQUE DE EL CAPRICHE

This is the closest Madrid comes to a formal English garden. Though a fair distance out, it's a pleasant place for a weekend stroll.

🗺 See map ▷ 99 ✉ Paseo de la Alameda de Osuna 🕐 Sat–Sun 9.30–6.30 🚇 El Capicho 🚌 101, 105, 115

PLAZA DE TOROS

las-ventas.com

This is the world's most important bullring, dating from 1930 and a fine example of neo-Mudéjar architecture. The museum here gives

you a basic overview of the famous names in bullfighting, if not the complex tradition of bullfighting itself.

🗺 M5 ✉ Avenida de los Tereros, Calle de Alcalá 237 ☎ Museum Taurino: 91 725 18 57. Stadium: 91 356 22 00 🕐 Museum Taurino: Mar–Oct Tue–Fri 9.30–2.30, Sun 10–1; Nov–Feb Mon–Fri 9.30–2.30 🚇 Ventas 🚌 12, 21, 38, 106, 110, 146 ♿ Very good 💶 Museum Taurino free

WARNER BROS PARK

parquewarner.com

This huge theme park on the outskirts of Madrid has five themed zones: Cartoon Village, Hollywood Boulevard, the Old West, Super Heroes and Warner Studios. Attractions include the Superman roller coaster with its seven loops, terrifying Batman ride and Yogi Bear water ride with water pistols.

🗺 See map ▷ 99 ✉ San Martín de La Vega. NIV to km22, then M-506 and follow signs ☎ 902 02 41 00 🕐 Hours vary 🍴 Cafés, restaurants 🚉 C3 from Atocha 🚌 412, 413 💶 Expensive

Plaza de Toros

Excursions

EL ESCORIAL

Felipe II's vast palace and monastery was built between 1563 and 1584 as his mausoleum. Apart from its political pedigree, it's also an architectural triumph, with impressive collections of objects and antiques.

The palace contains 16 courtyards, 2,673 windows, 1,200 doors and 86 staircases; 900m (2,952ft) of frescoes line the walls. Its power is breathtaking, and the clear mountain air has left its granite and blue roof slates looking extraordinarily new. Among the highlights are the monastery, the library and the mausoleum, the resting place of most Spanish monarchs since Carlos V (1500–58). There is also an impressive art collection: don't miss El Greco's *Adoration of the Name of Jesus* or the magnificent tapestries designed by Goya.

SEGOVIA

Segovia, perched on a lofty, rocky outcrop, was founded during the Iberian period and taken by the Romans in 80BC. Occupied by the Moors, it reverted to the Christians in 1085, and then prospered for centuries as a center for the textile industry. Now it is a popular weekend destination for *madrileños* in search of fresh air and a traditional suckling pig lunch: Segovia is known as the capital of Castillian cuisine.

The first thing you will see is the Roman aqueduct (first and second centuries AD), with 165 arches and a total length of 814m (2,670ft). In the old town are the magnificent 16th-century cathedral, with its imposing flying buttresses, and the 14th-century Alcázar, or fortress, which was largely rebuilt as a Gothic fantasy in the 19th century and offers lovely views from the top. Connecting these major sights, a warren of meandering streets pass by plazas, palaces, gardens and churches.

FARTHER AFIELD EXCURSIONS

TOLEDO

Legendary Toledo, with its hilltop site and fascinating maze of winding streets and hidden patios, is one of the nation's most beautiful and legendary cities. It was the Spanish capital from 567 to 711, and from 1085 to 1561. In other words, it has played a decisive role in Spanish history for far longer than Madrid.

National Monument Between the 12th and 15th centuries, Moors, Jews and Christians lived here side by side, and its rich combination of Moorish, Christian and Jewish heritage inspired its designation as a National Monument. Highlights are the 13th-century cathedral, the synagogues, Santo Tomé, the Museo de la Santa Cruz (for El Greco paintings) and the Alcázar, founded in 1085.

Alcázar Every culture that has ruled Toledo built a fortress on this site, and all dominated the city's skyline, as does the present-day version. This rather austere fortress was built by Carlos V in the 16th century. During the Civil War, owing to its strategic position, it endured a very destructive 70-day siege, and today it houses an army museum that concentrates on those dark days.

Catedral Toledo's cathedral, one of the world's finest Gothic buildings, took 267 years to erect (1226–1493). Among its treasures are a baroque marble, jasper and bronze altarpiece, and paintings by El Greco and Goya.

Judería Although only two of Toledo's original 10 synagogues stand today, there is still a surprising amount to see in the Jewish Quarter. The 14th-century Sinagoga del Tránsito, housing the Museo Sefardí, has a superb interior.

THE BASICS

toledo-turismo.com
Distance: 70km (45 miles)
Journey time: 1 hour 15 mins
🚌 Galeano International from Estación Sur, Méndez Álvaro
🚆 From Atocha, several every hour in summer, less frequent in winter. To avoid a steep climb take a bus up the hill
🛈 Paseo de la Rosa s/n (tel 92 524 82 32) open daily 9.30–3. There is a hop-on, hop-off tourist bus that leaves from outside the AVE station (€€€)

THE BASICS

aranjuez.com
Distance: 50km (31 miles)
Journey time: 1 hour
🚌 Estación Sur, Méndez Álvaro (tel 91 468 22 00)
🚆 Atocha (tel 902 24 02 02)
ℹ️ Plaza de San Antonio (tel 91 891 04 27). Open Tue–Sun 10–2, 4–6 (summer); 10–1, 3–5 (winter)

Palacio Real
☎ 91 891 07 40
🕐 Daily 10–6.15 (summer); 10–5.15 (winter).
💷 Moderate. Free Wed for EU citizens
❓ A special Strawberry Train (Tren de la Fresa) runs on weekends from Madrid, from late April through June. The train departs from Atocha train station at 10.05, arriving in Aranjuez at 11; the return journey departs around 6pm. The ticket price includes a guided visit of the palace and gardens, as well as a bowl of strawberries en route (tel 90 222 88 22; renfe.es)

ARANJUEZ

An hour south of Madrid is a city known as much for a piece of classical guitar music as for its glorious royal palace. On the banks of the Tajo River, Aranjuez is green, leafy and cool.

Palacio Real This lush landscape inspired Joaquín Rodrigo (1901–99) to compose the romantic and hugely popular Concierto de Aranjuez. (He is buried in the town cemetery.) The setting also drew Spanish rulers from the heat of Madrid. Although Felipe II commissioned the first palace back in 1561, the Palacio Real de Aranjuez took ages to finish: what you see is from the 18th century. But this fairy-tale palace was well worth the wait, from the throne room with its red velvet to the gala dining hall with its impressive chandeliers, furniture, tapestries and sculptures. One vast room, the Sala de Porcelana, is filled with porcelain, a particular hobby of Carlos III. Outstanding works of art include Murillo's *Bautismo de Cristo* (Baptism of Christ), which covers the ceiling of the chapel.

Gardens Many gardening enthusiasts go to Aranjuez just to see the landscaped grounds around the palace, with their fountains, statues and walks: the Jardín del Príncipe (Prince's Garden), the Jardín de Isabel II, the Jardín de la Isla (the Island) and the Jardín del Parterre, designed by Boutelou in 1746, with fine cedar trees, magnolias and flowers.

Strawberries The whole town is a pleasure to visit, with its old houses and small palaces, many of which are still in private hands. The town is also famous for its strawberries: a day trip to Aranjuez in early summer to eat strawberries is a Madrid tradition.

On a budget or celebrating a special event? With family or just looking for a fun weekend away? If you want to stay right in the throbbing heart of Madrid, there is accommodation for all budgets.

Introduction

Spain's capital has a wealth of hotels, *pensiones* and *hostales*. If you arrive without a booking, there are accommodation services at the airport and main bus and train stations. Many upper-range hotels, geared to business travel, offer reduced rates at weekends and holiday periods, so it's worth asking about reductions.

Location

The main factor to think about is location. The most popular area for visitors is in the heart of the old town (south of Sol between Plaza Mayor and Plaza de Santa Ana); you can walk to many of the main sights from here. Other options include Recoletos, the Paseo del Prado or Salamanca. If you want to be right in the heart of the nightlife action, Malasaña and Chueca are good bets.

Types of Accommodation

Spanish hotels are classified, regularly inspected and awarded 1 to 5 stars (*estrellas*). *Hostales* are often hard to distinguish from small hotels and can be better value for money. They are graded from 1 to 3 stars; a 3-star *hostal* is generally on a par with a 2-star hotel. *Pensiones* are usually family-run with simple rooms and sometimes shared bathrooms. Larger establishments have their own restaurants but in smaller places you'll need to eat out. If you prefer self-catering, you can also hire apartments from €50 a night for one person; see websites such as gomadrid.com or madridman.com. It's worth paying for a room with air conditioning; summer temperatures can exceed 40ºC (104ºF).

DISABLED ACCESS

Look for modern hotels if you require better access and specially adapted rooms (access-able.com). These range from the well-priced Ibis Centro, with two disabled rooms (ibis.com), to the luxury InterContinental Madrid (four rooms, ihg.com). The website laterooms.com lists rooms for people with disabilities. In Spanish, look for the word *minusválido* (disabled).

Budget Hotels

PRICES

Expect to pay up to €100 per night for two in a budget room.

HOSTAL CERVANTES

hostal-cervantes.com

Conveniently located on the street after which it is named, this is an easy walk from the Prado and Thyssen-Bornemisza. The 20 en-suite rooms are basic but clean and comfortable, with TVs, safes and hairdryers. The *hostal* is well located for tapas bars and cafés.

🔶 G8 ✉ Calle Cervantes 34 ☎ 91 429 83 65 🚇 Anton Martín, Banco de España

HOSTAL ORIENTE

hostaloriente.es

This excellent budget option has benefited from a contemporary update. All the rooms are individually decorated in tasteful earth colors offset by brightly patterned fabrics. The bathrooms are attractively tiled and some offer tubs as well as showers.

🔶 F7 ✉ Calle Arenal 23 ☎ 91 548 03 14 🚇 Ópera

IBIS MADRID CENTRO

ibishotel.com

On the site of a famous theater, this is a practical and friendly 64-room hotel in Malasaña, a good base location, with plenty of restaurants and bars nearby. Excellent breakfasts are served here.

🔶 F5 ✉ Calle de Manuela Malasaña 6 ☎ 91 448 58 16 🚇 Bilbao

MORA

hotelmora.com

The rooms here have been recently refurbished and updated. Some sport small balconies overlooking the elegant Paseo del Prado. Fortunately, double-glazing blocks out most of the traffic noise. The hotel is within walking distance of Atocha rail station.

🔶 G8 ✉ Paseo del Prado 32 ☎ 91 420 15 69 🚇 Atocha

ROOM MATE MARIO HOTEL

room-matehotels.com

Mario was the first of four brightly furnished budget hotels in the Room Mate hotel group. It is well situated close to the Teatro Real. Rooms are small but well equipped and the buffet breakfast is more generous than most.

🔶 E7 ✉ Calle de Campomanes 4 ☎ 91 548 85 48 🚇 Ópera

SAN LORENZO

hotel-sanlorenzo.com

This small hotel is well positioned for bars and restaurants and offers small, pristine rooms, simply decorated with warm wood furnishings. Several face an interior courtyard, while those overlooking the street are soundproofed.

🔶 G7 ✉ Calle Clavel 8 ☎ 91 521 30 57 🚇 Gran Vía

TRAFALGAR

hotel-trafalgar.com

The Trafalgar is in a residential area north of the center. All 48 rooms are decorated in modern style and have satellite TV. Facilities include a restaurant, bar and an indoor swimming pool.

🔶 F4 ✉ Calle Trafalgar 35 ☎ 91 445 62 00 🚇 Iglesia

HOSTELS

It is worth remembering that, at the lower end of the scale, a good *hostal* may be more comfortable than a poor hotel. Also bear in mind that prices can vary considerably according to season.

Mid-Range Hotels

PRICES
Expect to pay between €100 and €200 per night for two in a mid-range room.

ACIS Y GALATEA
hotelesglobales.com
This small and tasteful modern hotel lies outside the center in the direction of the airport and near the trade fair showground. As the name suggests, the interior decor is inspired by opera. Facilities include a roof terrace and pool.
➕ Off map ✉ Calle Galatea 6 ☎ 91 743 49 01 🚇 Canillejas

AROSA
hotelarosa.com
Very central, the 139-room Arosa has stylish and spacious rooms, some with private terraces. There is also a small fitness center.
➕ F7 ✉ Calle de la Salud 21 ☎ 91 532 16 00 🚇 Sol, Gran Vía

ARTRIP
artriphotel.com
This design-conscious hotel has large rooms, all eclectically decorated with a boho chic appeal. There are snacks and fresh fruit available to guests throughout the day, and the buffet breakfast is a notch above the norm.
➕ G9 ✉ Calle Valencia 11 ☎ 91 539 32 82 🚇 Lavapiés

ASTURIAS
hotel-asturias.com
A long-standing classic, the Asturias opened in 1875 and, despite the rather bland exterior, has plenty of charm. The rooms vary but are spacious and bright, with colorful fabrics and wooden fittings and floors. Ask for an interior room if you are sensitive to noise.
➕ G7 ✉ Calle Sevilla 2 ☎ 91 429 66 76 🚇 Sevilla

CONDE DUQUE
granhotelcondeduque.com
Located on a tranquil, tree-lined square, the 143-room Conde Duque is among the more peaceful hotels near the city center. Rooms are elegantly furnished and spacious.
➕ F5 ✉ Plaza del Conde Valle Suchil 5 ☎ 91 447 70 00 🚇 San Bernardo

EUROPA
hoteleuropa.eu
A comfortable hotel in a good location right on the Puerto del Sol, and within easy walking distance of the main sights, the Europa has recently refurbished rooms with pale-gray walls, crisp white linens and tasteful contemporary fabrics.
➕ F7 ✉ Calle del Carmen 4 ☎ 91 521 29 00 🚇 Callao

HOTEL T3 TIROL
t3tirol.com
A comfortable hotel in the Argüelles business district, this is also a good choice for families with small children. El Corte Inglés department store is just opposite, and Parque del Oeste is also nearby. The breakfast buffet is excellent, and there is parking.
➕ D5 ✉ Calle Marqués de Urquijo 4 ☎ 91 548 19 00 🚇 Argüelles

MEDIODÍA
mediodiahotel.com
Opposite Atocha train station, the Mediodía is close to the Reina Sofía and the Prado. The spacious, recently renovated rooms have large bathrooms and are tastefully decorated in cool colors.
➕ H9 ✉ Plaza Emperador Carlos V 8 ☎ 91 527 30 60 🚇 Atocha

MODERNO

hotel-moderno.com

This 3-star hotel on a pedestrian street is only moments away from the Plaza Mayor and the Puerta del Sol. The staff are particularly welcoming, and all 97 rooms have air-conditioning.

➕ F7 ✉ Calle del Arenal 2 ☎ 91 531 09 00 Ⓜ Sol

NH LAGASCA

nh-hotels.com

This 3-star hotel in the heart of the Salamanca district is near the Calle Serrano shops and many good restaurants. Its 100 rooms are plainly furnished with bright white fabrics, wooden floors and striking bathrooms. It also has parking.

➕ J5 ✉ Calle de Lagasca 64 ☎ 91 575 46 06 Ⓜ Velázquez, Serrano

OPERA

hotelopera.com

This slick, 79-room hotel has a great location near the opera house. Opt for a room with a terrace and Jacuzzi if you can. Other perks include a rooftop gym that offers superb views while you exercise, and a sauna.

➕ E7 ✉ Cuesta de Santo Domingo 2 ☎ 91 541 28 00 Ⓜ Ópera

RADISSON BLUE

radissonblue.com

This stylish hotel has a superb location across from Retiro park and offers rooms that are chic and contemporary, with a black and white color scheme, offset by edgy artwork on the walls. There are Nespresso machines and rain-head showers, and the hotel has a spa, indoor pool and whisky bar.

➕ G8 ✉ Calle de Moratín 52 ☎ 91 524 26 26 Ⓜ Atocha

SENATOR GRAN VÍA

hotelsenatorgranvia.com

This city hotel has an interior that blends functionality and urban style. The rooms are large and modern and several have superb Gran Vía views. The rooftop spa has a pool and Jacuzzi. The hotel also offers airport transfers.

➕ F7 ✉ Gran Vía 21 ☎ 91 531 41 51 Ⓜ Gran Vía

TRYP MADRID CHAMBERI

tryphotels.com

A 3-star, 72-room hotel with well-sized, air-conditioned rooms is in the affluent Chamberí area. Popular with business-people during the week, it offers attractive weekend rates for leisure visitors. It's well placed for the Real Madrid stadium and there's parking nearby.

➕ F3 ✉ José Abascal 8 ☎ 91 447 40 00 Ⓜ Canal, Alonso Cano, Río Rosas

VINCCI SOHO

vinccihoteles.com

Located in the heart of happening Huertas, this is one of the city's latest hotels. It is chic and stylish, with large, light rooms, bold fabrics and plenty of shiny wood. There are coffee makers in the rooms.

➕ G8 ✉ Called del Prado 18 ☎ 91 141 41 00 Ⓜ Antón Martín

ZENIT ABEBA

hotelzenitabeba.zenithoteles.com

This modern 4-star hotel is perfect for shoppers as it is just a stone's throw from Goya and Serrano streets. The decor is functional, but the rooms are comfortable and spacious. The restaurant serves traditional Spanish cuisine and opens for lunch and dinner.

➕ K5 ✉ Calle de Alcántara 63 ☎ 91 401 16 50 Ⓜ Diego de León

Luxury Hotels

CASA DE MADRID

casademadrid.com

A short walk from the Royal Palace, this exclusive hotel is owned by art historian and interior designer Marta Medina Muro. Each of the seven rooms is exquisitely decorated and furnished.

🞧 E7 ✉ Calle Arrieta 2 ☎ 91 559 57 91 🚇 Ópera

HOSPES PUERTA DE ALCALÁ

hospes.com

A romantic boutique hotel in a classic 1883 building with beautifully designed rooms, Hospes is in walking distance of Madrid's major museums and shopping.

🞧 H7 ✉ Plaza de la Independencia 3 ☎ 91 432 29 11 🚇 Retiro, Banco de España

HOTEL PUERTA AMÉRICA

hotelpuertamerica.com

This Silken hotel boasts 12 floors of vibrant colors, each designed by a diferent architect, a rooftop bar, black swimming pool and imaginative restaurant. It's not central, but close to Calle de Serrano shopping.

🞧 L3 ✉ Avenida de América 41 ☎ 91 744 54 00 🚇 Cartagena

HOTEL URBAN

derbyhotels.com

The hard edges of this contemporary retreat next to the Parliament building are softened by original and ancient works of art. The 96 designer bedrooms have all the latest gadgets. The Glass Bar (▷ 64) is a popular rendezvous.

🞧 G7 ✉ Carrera de San Jerónimo 34 ☎ 91 787 77 70 🚇 Sol, Sevilla

INTERCONTINENTAL MADRID

ihg.com/intercontinental

Grand and central, with lots of marble and glass, this is where businesspeople and celebrities stay. Rooms and bathrooms are spacious and comfortable. In summer, the courtyard garden restaurant has live music. The weekend rates are attractive.

🞧 H4 ✉ Paseo de la Castellana 49 ☎ 91 700 73 00 🚇 Gregorio Marañón

ME MADRID

mebymelia.com

Once the formal old Reina Victoria (where bullfighters always stayed), this grand hotel has all the usual luxuries, from 300-thread-count linen and down pillow-top mattresses to organic, all-natural products for the shower.

🞧 F8 ✉ Plaza de Santa Ana 14 ☎ 91 701 60 00 🚇 Anton Martín

RITZ

ritzmadrid.com

Spain's first luxury hotel, opened in 1910, was built for King Alfonso XIII. It lives up to its name, with 167 luxurious rooms in belle époque style. Between spring and fall there's a delightful terrace-restaurant. Afternoon tea, taken to the sounds of a pianist, harpist or classical guitarist, is a highlight.

🞧 H7 ✉ Plaza de la Lealtad 5 ☎ 91 901 67 67 🚇 Banco de España

Madrid is easy to get to from anywhere
in the world. Although very walkable, the
city also has excellent public transport.
The main thing is to understand the hours
when *madrileños* work, eat and play.

Need to Know

Planning Ahead

When to Go

Because of its position high on the inland plateau, Madrid can have some of the most extreme weather conditions in central Spain. Spring, early summer and autumn are the best times to visit. Tourist crowds dwindle in winter, when the weather can be bitterly cold, with temperatures rarely above freezing during the day, and icy after dark.

TIME

Spain is six hours ahead of New York, nine hours ahead of Los Angeles, and one hour ahead of the UK.

AVERAGE DAILY MAXIMUM TEMPERATURES											
JAN	FEB	MAR	APR	MAY	JUN	JUL	AUG	SEP	OCT	NOV	DEC
48°F	52°F	59°F	63°F	70°F	79°F	88°F	86°F	77°F	66°F	55°F	48°F
9°C	11°C	15°C	17°C	21°C	26°C	31°C	30°C	25°C	19°C	13°C	9°C

Spring (March to mid-June) vies with fall as the most pleasant time of year, with clear skies and sunny days, though there may be showers.
Summer (mid-June to August) is hot and dry. Rain is unusual between June and October. July and August are particularly hot.
Autumn (September to October) has little rain, sunny days and moderate temperatures.
Winter (November to February) has dry, clear days and low temperatures.

WHAT'S ON

January Cabalgata de Reyes (5 Jan): A procession marks the Three Wise Men's arrival. San Antón (17 Jan): Pets are blessed in the San Antón Church, Calle Hortaleza 63.
February Carnival: A week of processions and parties ends on Ash Wednesday with the ritual "Burial of the Sardine" by the River Manzanares. ARCO: International contemporary arts festival.
April Semana Santa (Holy Week): Hooded, shoeless, chain-dragging penitentes bear images of Christ and the Virgin on their shoulders.

On Holy Thursday, during the procession around La Latina, the entire barrio takes to the streets.
May Labor Day and Madrid Day (1–2 May): Concerts region-wide; the main venue is Plaza Mayor. San Isidro (15 May): Nightly concerts in Plaza Mayor mark the week leading up to the saint's day of San Isidro.
June San Antonio de la Florida (13 Jun): Street party marks St. Antonio's feast day. San Juan (23 Jun): Fireworks in the Retiro to celebrate the festival of St. John.

August Veranos de la Villa: Madrid's summer festival of music, dance, theater and more.
October Festival de Otoño: International performing arts festival (through November).
November International Jazz Festival: Venues all over the city.
December Fiestas de Navidad: Christmas lights, markets and crèches lead up to Christmas. Christmas fair in Plaza Mayor. New Year's Eve: Thousands gather for the fireworks in the Puerta del Sol.

Madrid Online

spain.info
The official website for tourism in Spain, with pages in Spanish, English, German, French, Italian, Japanese and Chinese. Easy to navigate, with plenty of useful information.

spain.info/en_US
Aimed at the US market, this offshoot of the main portal has plenty of information, plus details of travel agents and tour operators that are Spain specialists. It also lists all the Spanish tourist offices in the United States.

turismomadrid.es
The official site of the Comunidad de Madrid, the autonomous Region of Madrid. In Spanish and English, with pages in other languages, it also covers nearby excursion destinations such as Segovia, San Lorenzo de El Escorial and Toledo. Your best introduction to the city.

gomadrid.com
An extensive guide to the city, including accommodations, tours, restaurants and sights, including any discounts available, plus useful listings of what's on right now.

thelocal.es
News and current affairs about Spain, in English. The website also has a classified ads section that includes information about finding employment in Spain.

ctm-madrid.es
Come to terms with getting around Madrid by browsing the official transport site covering buses and the Metro (in English).

lecool.com
This is an alternative website to what is going on in Madrid, concentrating on the quirky, off-beat and avant-garde. There are sections on restaurants, hotels and shops, as well as cool activities to do with kids.

TRAVEL SITES

fodors.com
A complete travel-planning site. You can research prices and weather; book air tickets, cars, and rooms; ask questions (and get answers) from fellow travelers; and find links to other sites.

renfe.es
The official site of Spanish National Railways, with an English-language option.

wunderground.com
American website providing comprehensive global weather forecasts.

WIFI

There are WiFi hotspots all over the city. An ever-increasing number of cafés and restaurants also offer free WiFi to customers, as do the vast majority of hotels, including the humblest establishments.

Getting There

- Anyone entering Spain must have a valid passport (or official identity card for EU nationals). Visa requirements are subject to change; check before making your reservations.
- Passengers on all flights to and from Spain have to supply advance passenger information (API) to the Spanish authorities. Full names, nationality, date of birth and travel document details (a passport number), are required. This information is compulsory and will be requested by the airline when you book your flight to Spain.

- The limits for non-EU visitors are 200 cigarettes or 50 cigars, or 250g of tobacco; 1 liter of spirits (over 22 percent) or 2 liters of fortified wine, 2 liters of still wine; 50ml of perfume. Travelers under 18 are not entitled to the tobacco and alcohol allowances.
- The guidelines for EU residents (for personal use) are 800 cigarettes, 200 cigars, 1kg tobacco; 10 liters of spirits (over 22 percent), 20 liters of aperitifs, 90 liters of wine, of which 60 can be sparkling wine, 110 liters of beer.

All flights arrive at Madrid-Barajas Airport, 12km (7.5 miles) northeast of the city. There are four terminals: T1, T2, T3 and the newest, T4, which is used by major international airlines such as Iberia and British Airways. For more information on arrivals and departures from each of the terminals, go to aena-aeropuertos.es (tel 902 40 47 04).

ARRIVING BY AIR

There are tourist information areas at the airport and leaflets with information about getting to Madrid from Barajas. All terminals are served by Metro station Aeropuerto (Line 8); trains run from 6am to 1.30am. Terminal one is a long walk from the Metro station so allow 10 minutes to reach it. All terminals are linked by the free AENA (airport) shuttle bus; transit time between terminals ranges from 2–8 minutes. A taxi from the airport to the middle of Madrid takes around 30 minutes and costs €25–€40. For more information on ground transport, look at aena-aeropuertos.es and metromadrid.es.

ARRIVING BY TRAIN

RENFE (renfe.es), Spain's national rail company, has two mainline stations in the city. Trains from northern Europe, France and Barcelona (including the high-speed AVE train) arrive on the north side of the city at Chamartín. Trains running to and from Portugal and the south of Spain (including the high-speed AVE train) use Atocha, close to the city center. Book direct on

renfe.com or use RENFE's US agents (Palace Tours, 800-724-5120, palacetours.com/renfe). Booking direct is preferable and the RENFE site is explained at seat61.com. For more information, see turismomadrid.es and esmadrid.com.

ARRIVING BY BUS
Madrid is served from other parts of Spain by many private bus companies. Inter-city coach services arrive at the Estación Sur de Autobuses on Calle Méndez Alvaro, southeast of the city center. Buses from outside Spain also terminate here. For all bus information, check estaciondeautobuses.com.

ARRIVING BY CAR
Drivers access Madrid via the Spanish system of toll motorways (*autopistas*) or highways (*autovías*). From France and the north, routes run along both the Mediterranean and Atlantic coasts then head toward Madrid; routes through the Pyrenees are slower but more scenic. Madrid is clearly signposted at all interchanges. From southern Spain, take the A-4 from Seville via Córdoba. From Portugal take the A-5 from Badajoz. All roads connect with the three ring roads circling Madrid: the M30, M40 and M45. Head for Paseo de la Castellana, Madrid's main artery—most central locations are easily reached from here.

SENSIBLE PRECAUTIONS
● Carry valuables in a belt, pouch or similar—not in a pocket. Be especially wary in the crowds around Plaza Mayor, Puerta del Sol and the Rastro market.
● Do not keep valuables in the front section of your rucksack. If possible, wear your rucksack on your front on buses and trains.
● Be aware of street tricks around tourist attractions, where one person distracts you in conversation, or offers to help you with something, while someone else grabs your bag.
● Don't take photos of street performers without their permission.

INSURANCE
Check your insurance coverage and buy a supplementary policy if necessary. EU nationals receive medical treatment with the EHIC (European Health Insurance Card), which should be obtained before traveling. Health and travel insurance is still advised.

VISITORS WITH A DISABILITY
General access in Madrid is patchy, but gradually improving. For getting around, buses and taxis are the best bet, although only the newest buses have facilities for people with disabilities. New buildings and museums have excellent wheelchair access, older attractions have yet to be converted, and churches are particularly difficult. FAMMA is the Spanish association that deals with all disabilities (in Spanish only, famma.org). There is also some limited information in English on the local authority's website: esmadrid.com/en/accessible-madrid.

Getting Around

Metro maps are available from the ticket counter. Free maps of the city are readily available at tourist offices, hotels, train stations and the airport.
Metro platforms have street maps indicating which exit leads where.

BUSES

● The bus system is efficient and far-reaching, with regular scheduled services to all parts of the city and its suburbs.

● Finding your way is made easy, as the various routes and stops are shown on a plan at every bus stop.

● There are two types of buses—the standard red bus and the yellow microbus. Both operate between 6am and midnight, and charge €1.50 for each one-way ride in the city, though the *abono* or Metrobus ticket, allowing 10 rides, costs €12.20 (see below).

● Night buses (known locally as *búhos*, meaning owls) operate from Plaza de Cibeles to many suburbs between midnight and 6am and the tickets cost the same as during the day. The night bus service is not as punctual as the daytime one.

● Bus information offices are located in Plaza de Cibeles and Puerta del Sol, where you can pick up route maps and schedules.

● For full bus information, see emtmadrid.es.

METRO

● The Metro system is very reliable and the best way of getting around the city quickly.

● There are 13 lines, each with a different color and number shown on route maps and at stations.

● The Metro is constantly expanding and improving. Most of the new stations are on the outskirts of this fast-growing city, built to speed commuters to and from work. The Metro is clean and safe for visitors.

● The system is split into zones, with most of it in Zone A, and the outlying areas and lines in zones B1, B2 and B3.

● The two airport terminals are classed as a separate zone, for which a supplementary fee is charged.

● A single journey ticket (*sencilla*) within Zone A costs €1.50 (€2 for all zones), but you can get a Metrobus ticket, giving 10 rides, for €12.20.

● A tourist card (*abono turistico*) for 1, 2, 3, 5 or 7 days is also available for visitors. A 1-day pass costs €8.40 for Zone A, a 7-day pass €35.40, with reductions of up to 50 percent for children. You would need to make six Metro or bus trips a day for it to work out cheaper than a Metrobus ticket.

● Buy tickets (also valid for buses) from Metro stations, some newsagents and tobacconists.

● The Metro system runs from 6am to 2am; schedule information and a full Metro map are available from metromadrid.es (tel 902 44 44 03), or from any station. Also see ctm-madrid. es, which has all the information in English as well as Spanish.

● Metro trains run about every 3 to 6 minutes from Monday to Friday; this extends to every 15 minutes after midnight, and there are slightly fewer trains on weekends.

● It's best to avoid the rush hours, generally 7–9.30am and 6–8pm, when it gets very busy.

TAXIS

● Official taxis are white with a diagonal red stripe. A green light on the roof shows when they are free.

● The standard base taxi fare is €2.40, with a charge of €1 for every further kilometer. There is a supplement payable on Sundays and holidays, and for certain destinations, such as the rail station, airport and bullring.

● Make sure the meter is turned on and set at the base fare for your journey.

● The major private taxi companies in Madrid are TeleTaxi (tel 91 371 21 31) and Radio Taxi (tel 91 447 32 32). You can book your taxi online at radiotaxigremial.com.

TRAINS

● Chamartín, north of Plaza de Castilla, is the terminus for northern destinations. It is linked by a through line with Atocha.

● *Cercanías* refers to local and suburban trains, *largo recorrido* to intercity and long-distance trains.

GUIDED TOURS

Enjoy wine tasting, gourmet tapas or a cookery class organized by Gourmet Madrid Tours. They also offer a day of wine tasting in Toledo and personalized tours (☎ 91 771 02 16; gourmetmadrid.com).

Now Europe wide, Sandeman offers free and paying walking tours of Madrid with several themes available, including the Spanish Inquisition, Majestic Madrid, Tapas and Madrid Night Out. Tours run for roughly 2.5 hours (new-europetours.eu).

For a really special experience, get under the skin of Madrid on a tour run by LeTango Tours. They take you to the places that locals go, explaining how various traditions began and why they persist. One of the most entertaining walks is a foodie-oriented tapas tour (☎ 655 818 740, mobile 661 752 458, toll free US 1 866 866 5107; letango.com).

A British guide with a passion for the Duke of Wellington, Stephen Drake-Jones also runs the Wellington Society, devoted to understanding the history of Spain in general and Madrid in particular (mobile 609 143 203; wellsoc.org).

Essential Facts

NEED TO KNOW ESSENTIAL FACTS

LOST AND FOUND

● Municipal Lost Property Office (Oficina de Objetos Perdidos) ✉ Paseo del Molino 7 ☎ 91 527 95 90 Ⓜ Legazpi 🕐 Mon–Fri 9–2

● For objects lost on a bus: EMT ✉ Cerro de la Plata 4 ☎ 902 50 78 50 Ⓜ Pacífico 🕐 Mon–Fri 9–2. Ask for *objetos perdidos*.

● To claim insurance, you must obtain a *denuncia* (signed statement of loss) from a police station.

MONEY

The euro (€) is the official currency of Spain. Banknotes are in denominations of 5, 10, 20, 50, 100, 200 and 500 euros, and coins in denominations of 1, 2, 5, 10, 20, 50 cents and 1 and 2 euros.

TOILETS

Gone are the days when tourists needed to worry; modern Spain has modern toilet facilities.

ELECTRICITY

● The standard current is 220 volts.
● Plugs are of the round two-pin type.

ETIQUETTE

● Spaniards rarely form orderly lines, but are generally aware of their place in the service order nevertheless.

● Smoking is officially banned in all enclosed public spaces in Spain, including hotels, bars and restaurants.

● It is considered good manners to issue a general hello (*buenos días* in the morning; *buenas tardes* in the afternoon/evening) when entering a shop, office, etc. and to say goodbye (*adios*) when leaving.

● Speak up to attract attention when you want to be served in bars and restaurants. Say *Oiga* (Oy-ga, literally "hear me"), and add *por favor* (please).

● When at a bar, expect to pay for your drinks before you leave the bar, not on a round-by-round basis.

● Tipping is discretionary, but 5 percent is normal practice.

MONEY MATTERS

● Most major travelers' checks can be changed at banks. American Express offers the best travelers' check rates.

● Credit cards are generally accepted in all large establishments and also in many smaller places.

● There are numerous multilingual ATM/cash machines.

OPENING HOURS

● Shops: 9–1.30, 5–8; department stores: 9–9. Some are open Sundays.

● Churches: 9.30–1.30, 5–7.30. Many only open half an hour before a service.

● Museums: many close on Mondays.

● Banks: Mon–Fri 9–2; between October and May many banks open also from 9–1 on Saturdays.

MAIL

● Buy stamps (*sellos*) from a post office (*oficina de Correos*) or tobacconists (*estancos*), indicated by a yellow and brown sign.

● Madrid's most central post office is at Paseo del Prado 1 (tel 91 523 06 94), open Mon–Fri 8.30am–9.30pm Sat 8.30–2. There are other post offices at El Corte Ingles, Calle Preciados 1–4, Carrera de San Francisco 13 and Calle Jorge Juan 20.

● Post boxes are mostly yellow with two slots, one marked "Madrid" and the other for every-where else (*Provincias y extranjero*).

TELEPHONES

● Public telephones take €1 and €2 coins and 2c, 5c, 10c, 20c and 50c coins.

● Phone cards are available from newsstands; some phones accept credit cards.

● The technology for mobile, or cell, phones in Spain is GSM, which may be incompatible with some countries, for example, the USA or Japan. Tri-band mobiles/cell phones will work. Check to make sure your phone will work and what the cost of calls will be—roaming charges can be high outside the EU.

● To call Spain from the UK, dial 00 34 followed by 91 for Madrid and then the seven-digit number. To call the UK from Spain, dial 00 44 and omit the zero from the area code. To call Australia, dial 00 61.

● To call Spain from the US, dial 011 34 fol-lowed by 91 for Madrid and then the seven-digit number. To call the US from Spain, dial 001.

MEDICINES AND HEALTHCARE

● Pharmacies (*farmacias*) are indicated by a flashing green cross and are usually open 9.30–2 and 5–8. All post a list of *farmacias de guardia* (all-night chemists).

● Spanish pharmacists are qualified to give over-the-counter advice on healthcare and minor ailments, but for serious conditions, ask for directions to the nearest hospital or doctor.

EMERGENCY NUMBERS

● Police (Local) 092
● Police (National) 091
● Police (Guardia Civil) 062
● Police, Ambulance, Fire 112
● Fire station: Madrid ☎ 080
● SATE is a special 24-hour service for tourists who need to report crimes. In Spanish, English and French ☎ 90 210 21 12; es.madrid.com.

TOURIST OFFICES

Plaza Mayor 27 ☎ 91 454 44 10 Ⓓ Daily 9.30–8.30
Plaza de Colón ✉ Access through Paseo de la Castellana Ⓓ Daily 9.30–8.30
Plaza de Cibeles ✉ Calle Bulevar (on corner with Paseo del Prado) Ⓓ Daily 9.30–8.30
Paseo de Arte ✉ On corner with Glorieta de Carlos V Ⓓ Daily 9.30–8.30
Madrid-Barajas Airport Terminal 2 and 4 ☎ 91 305 86 56 Ⓓ Daily 10am–11pm
Terminal 4 ☎ 902 10 00 07 Ⓓ Daily 10am–11pm esmadrid.com

Language

English is now the second language of many, if not most, Europeans. Staff in Madrid's hotels, restaurants and even shops will speak English. However, it is fun to try a few words in Spanish and, of course, any efforts are appreciated! In bars, the tapas on offer are often chalked up on a board; perfect for trying out your Spanish.

Pronunciation
c before an *e* or an *i*, and *z* are like *th* in thin
c in other cases is like *c* in cat
g before an *e* or an *i*, and *j* are a guttural sound which does not exist in English—rather like the *ch* in loch
g in other cases is like *g* in get
h is normally silent
ll is similar to y
y is like the *i* in onion
Use the formal *usted* when speaking to strangers; the informal *tu* for friends or younger people.

COURTESIES	
good morning	*buenos días*
good afternoon/ evening	*buenas tardes*
good night	*buenas noches*
hello (informal)	*hola*
goodbye (informal)	*hasta luego/hasta pronto*
hello (answering the phone)	*¿Diga?*
goodbye	*adiós*
please	*por favor*
thank you	*gracias*
you're welcome	*de nada*
how are you? (formal)	*¿Como está?*
how are you? (informal)	*¿Que tal?*
I'm fine	*estoy bien*
I'm sorry	*lo siento*
excuse me (in a bar)	*oiga*
excuse me (in a crowd)	*perdón*

USEFUL WORDS	
I don't know	*No lo sé*
I don't think so	*Creo que no*
I think so	*Creo que sí*
It doesn't matter	*No importa*
Where?	*¿Dónde?*
When?	*¿Cuándo?*
Why?	*¿Por qué?*
What?	*¿Qué?*
Who?	*¿Quién?*
How?	*¿Cómo?*
How much/ many?	*¿Cuánto/ cuántos?*
Is/are there?	*¿Hay?*
ticket	*entrada*

BASIC VOCABULARY

yes/no	*sí/no*
I do not understand	*no entiendo*
left/right	*izquierda/derecha*
entrance/exit	*entrada/salida*
open/closed	*abierto/cerrado*
good/bad	*bueno/malo*
big/small	*grande/pequeño*
with/without	*con/sin*
more/less	*más/menos*
hot/cold	*caliente/frío*
early/late	*temprano/tarde*
here/there	*aquí/allí*
today/tomorrow	*hoy/mañana*
yesterday	*ayer*
how much is it?	*¿cuánto es?*
where is the...?	*¿dónde está...?*
do you have...?	*¿tiene...?*
I'd like...	*me gustaría...*
I don't speak Spanish	*no hablo español*

FOOD

apple	*manzana*
banana	*plátano*
beans	*habichuelas*
chicken	*pollo*
clams	*almejas*
duck	*pato*
fish/	*pescado/*
seafood	*marisco*
fruit	*fruta*
lamb	*cordero*
lettuce	*lechuga*
lobster	*langosta*
meat	*carne*
melon	*melón*
orange	*naranja*
pork	*cerdo*
shrimp	*gambas*
squid	*calamares*
tomato	*tomate*
tuna	*atún*
turkey	*pavo*

IN THE RESTAURANT

smoking allowed	*se permite fumar*
no smoking	*se prohibe fumar*
menu	*la carta*
fork	*tenedor*
knife	*cuchillo*
spoon	*cuchara*
napkin	*servilleta*
glass of wine	*copa*
glass of beer	*caña*
water (mineral)	*agua (mineral)*
still	*sin gas*
sparkling/bubbles	*con gas*
coffee (with milk)	*café (con leche)*
The bill/check, please	*¿La cuenta, por favor?*
Do you take credit cards?	*¿Aceptan tarjetas de crédito?*
tavern	*mesón/taberna*
cakes	*pasteles*
small snacks	*pinchos*
sandwiches	*bocadillos*
set dishes	*platos combinados*

SHOPPING

ATM/cash machine	*cajero*
I want to buy…	*Quiero comprar…*
belt	*cinturón*
blouse	*blusa*
dress	*vestido*
shirt	*camisa*
shoes	*zapatas*
skirt	*falda*
tie	*corbata*
gloves	*guantes*
socks	*calcetines*
small	*pequeño*
medium	*mediano*
large	*grande*
cotton	*algodón*
silk	*seda*
wool	*lana*
café	*cafetería*
breakfast	*desayuno*
lunch	*almuerzo*
dinner	*cena*

Timeline

BEFORE AD800

Iberian tribes inhabited Madrid from around 1000BC. The Romans ruled the Iberian peninsula between 218BC and the 5th century AD and Madrid became a stopping place. In AD711, Muslims defeated the Visigoths and areas of Spain came under Muslim rule for 800 years.

854 Muhammad I of Córdoba founds the city of Madrid.

1083 Madrid is recaptured by Alfonso VI; Christians, Jews and Muslims all inhabit the city.

1202 Alfonso VIII recognizes Madrid as a city by giving it Royal Statutes.

1309 The Cortes, or Parliament, meets in Madrid for the first time.

1469 The marriage of the Catholic monarchs Ferdinand and Isabella unites Aragon and Castile.

1492 The conquest of Granada completes the unification of Spain. Spain begins a 200-year period of imperial power, and expels the Jews.

1561 Felipe II establishes his court in Madrid: a cultural "Golden Age" begins.

1578 Felipe III (1578–1621) is the first monarch to be born in Madrid.

1617–19 Plaza Mayor is built.

1759 Carlos III begins a modernization schedule for Madrid.

1808–12 French occupation; famine kills 30,000. Spanish rule restored in 1814.

Below, from left to right: Queen Isabella receives Christopher Columbus; Ferdinand the Catholic; Felipe II; statue of Felipe III in the Plaza Mayor; General Francisco Franco; statue of the painter Goya

1819 Prado museum opens.

1873 The First Republic is declared.

1919 The first Metro line in Madrid opens.

1931 The Second Republic is declared.

1936–39 The Spanish Civil War takes place, sparked by an uprising in North Africa. The Nationalists win, and the long dictatorship of General Franco follows.

1975 General Franco dies; King Juan Carlos is declared his successor.

1977 The first democratic general election.

1986 Spain joins the EEC (now EU).

1992 Madrid is European City of Culture.

2002 Spain adopts the euro.

2008–14 Despite recession, Madrid commits to a "greener" future with the Madrid Río project, a new 10km (6.4-mile) long park along the Manzanares river.

2014 Juan Carlos abdicates the throne and his son becomes Felipe VI.

2016 Mariano Rajoy, leader of the conservartive People's Party, returns to office to avoid a third election.

MADRID PEOPLE

Carlos III
Carlos III is often known as "the best mayor that Madrid ever had". More than any other single historical figure, he is responsible for today's Madrid. He came to the throne in 1759 and was a keen proponent of Enlightenment ideals.

Cervantes
Cervantes is the author of *Don Quixote,* believed by some to be the first novel ever written. A tax collector, he wrote *Don Quixote* while in jail for manipulating accounts. He died in Madrid in 1616.

Goya
Goya (1746–1828) is the painter most readily associated with Madrid, though he was neither born here nor died here. He settled in Madrid in 1774 and became court painter to Carlos IV in 1789.

Index

CityPack Madrid

Published by AA Publishing, a trading name of AA Media Limited, whose registered office is Fanum House, Basing View, Basingstoke, Hampshire RG21 4EA. Registered number 06112600.

© AA Media Limited 2018
First published 1997
New editions 2015 and 2018

Written by Jonathan Holland
Additional writing Paul Wade and Kathy Arnold
Updated by Josephine Quintero
Series editor Clare Ashton
Design work Tom Whitlock and Liz Baldin
Image retouching and repro Ian Little

Colour separation by AA Digital Department
Printed and bound by Leo Paper Products, China

A CIP catalogue record for this book is available from the British Library.

ISBN 978-0-7495-7977-7

A05593
Maps in this title produced from mapping © MAIRDUMONT / Falk Verlag 2015 and data from openstreetmap.org © OpenStreetMap contributors
Transport map © Communicarta Ltd, UK

The Automobile Association would like to thank the following photographers, companies and picture libraries for their assistance in the preparation of this book.

2 AA/M Jourdan; 3 AA/M Jourdan; 4t AA/M Jourdan; 4c AA/M Jourdan; 5t AA/M Jourdan; 5c © Palacio Nacional; 6t AA/M Jourdan; 6cl AA/R Strange; 6cr AA/M Chaplow; 6bl AA/M Chaplow; 6bc AA/M Jourdan; 6br AA/S Day; 7t AA/M Jourdan; 7cl AA/M Jourdan; 7cr AA/C Sawyer; 7bl AA/M Chaplow; 7br AA/M Jourdan; 8 AA/M Jourdan; 9 AA/M Jourdan; 10t AA/M Jourdan; 10ct AA/M Jourdan; 10c AA/M Chaplow; 10cb AA/M Jourdan; 10/11 AA/M Jourdan; 11t AA/M Jourdan; 11ct AA/M Jourdan; 11c AA/R Strange; 11cb AA/M Chaplow; 12t AA/M Jourdan; 12b AA/R Strange; 13t AA/M Jourdan; 13ct AA/M Jourdan; 13c AA/M Chaplow; 13cb AA/M Jourdan; 13b AA/M Jourdan; 14t AA/M Jourdan; 14cr AA/M Jourdan; 14c AA/M Chaplow; 14cb AA/M Jourdan; 14b AA/M Chaplow; 15t AA/M Jourdan; 15b AA/M Chaplow; 16t AA/M Jourdan; 16ct AA/M Chaplow; 16c AA/M Chaplow; 16b AA/J Edmanson; 17t AA/M Jourdan; 17ct Maria Galan/Alamy Stock Photo; 17c AA/M Chaplow; 17b AA/J Tims; 18t AA/M Jourdan; 18ct AA/M Chaplow; 18c AA/C Sawyer; 18cb Photodisc; 18b Brand X Pictures; 19i AA/M Jourdan; 19ii AA/M Jourdan; 19iii AA/M Jourdan; 19iv AA/R Strange; 19v AA/M Chaplow; 20/21 AA/M Jourdan; 24l AA/M Chaplow; 24r AA/M Jourdan; 25l AA/R Strange; 25c AA/R Strange; 25r AA/M Jourdan; 26l AA/M Chaplow; 26r AA/R Strange; 27l AA/M Chaplow; 27r AA/P Enticknap; 28 Courtesy of Museum Cerralbo; 28/29 Courtesy of Museo Cerralbo; 30l AA/R Strange; 30r AA/R Strange; 31l Courtesy of Museo Traje; 31r Courtesy of Museo Traje; 32 AA/M Jourdan; 32/33t AA/M Jourdan; 32/33b AA/M Jourdan; 33t AA/M Chaplow; 33cl AA/M Jourdan; 33cr AA/M Jourdan; 34l AA/R Strange; 34r AA/R Strange; 35l AA/M Chaplow; 35c AA/M Chaplow; 35r AA/M Chaplow; 36t AA/M Jourdan; 36b AA/M Jourdan; 37t AA/M Jourdan; 37b Peter Domotor/Alamy Stock Photo; 38 AA/M Jourdan; 39 AA/R Strange; 40 AA/M Jourdan; 41 ImageState; 42 ImageState; 43 AA/R Strange; 46 Joaquín Cortes/ Román Lores; 47l Joaquín Cortes/Román Lores; 47cr Joaquín Cortes/Román Lores; 47tr Joaquín Cortes/Román Lores; 48 AA/M Chaplow; 48/49 AA/M Jourdan; 50l AA/R Strange; 50r AA/M Chaplow; 51l AA/M Jourdan; 51c AA/M Jourdan; 51r AA/M Chaplow; 52l Peter M. Wilson/Alamy Stock Photo; 52r Anastasiya Piatrova; 53l AA/M Jourdan; 53c AA/M Chaplow; 53r AA/M Chaplow; 54r AA/M Jourdan; 54l AA/M Jourdan; 55 Alex Segre / Alamy Stock Photo Stock Photo Stock Photo; 56t AA/M Jourdan; 56b AA/M Jourdan; 57t AA/M Jourdan; 57b AA/M Chaplow; 58t AA/M Jourdan; 58bl AA/M Chaplow; 58br Peter Eastland/Alamy; 59t AA/M Jourdan; 59b AA/J Edmanson; 60 AA/M Jourdan; 61 AA/R Strange; 62 AA/R Strange; 63 AA/M Jourdan; 64 AA/M Jourdan; 65 ImageState; 66 ImageState; 67 AA/J Edmanson; 70 Adam Eastland/Alamy Stock Photo; 71 Adam Eastland/Alamy Stock Photo; 73 AA/M Jourdan; 72 AA/M Jourdan; 74 AA/M Jourdan; 75l AA/M Chaplow; 75r AA/M Chaplow; 76/7 AA/M Jourdan; 77t AA/M Jourdan; 77c Fernando Cortés de Pablo / Alamy Stock Photo; 78t AA/M Jourdan; 78bl AA/M Chaplow; 78br AA/M Chaplow; 79t AA/M Jourdan; 79b AA/M Chaplow; 80 AA/R Strange; 81t AA/M Jourdan; 81c ImageState; 82 ImageState; 83 AA/R Strange; 86 INTERFOTO / Alamy Stock Photo; 86/87 Bridgeman; 88 AA/M Chaplow; 88/89 AA/R Strange; 90t AA/M Jourdan; 90b Juan Lazo Zbikowski / Alamy Stock Photo; 91t AA/M Jourdan; 91b AA/M Chaplow; 92t AA/M Jourdan; 92b AA/R Strange; 93 AA/M Jourdan; 94 AA/R Strange; 95 AA/M Jourdan; 96 ImageState; 97 Robert Harding/Alamy Stock Photo; 100l AA/M Chaplow; 100r AA/M Chaplow; 101t AA/M Jourdan; 101b AA/C Sawyer; 102t AA/M Jourdan; 102b Robert Harding/Alamy Stock Photo; 103t AA/M Chaplow; 103lbl AA/M Chaplow; 103bl AA/M Chaplow; 103br AA/M Chaplow; 103rbr AA/M Chaplow; 104 AA/M Chaplow; 105t AA/M Chaplow; 105bl AA/M Chaplow; 105bc AA/M Chaplow; 105br AA/M Chaplow; 106t AA/M Chaplow; 106bl AA/J Edmanson; 106bc AA/J Edmanson; 106br AA/J Edmanson; 107 AA/C Sawyer; 108t AA/C Sawyer; 108ct Photodisc; 108c Photodisc; 108cb Photodisc; 108b Stockbyte; 109 AA/C Sawyer; 110 AA/C Sawyer; 111 AA/C Sawyer; 112 AA/C Sawyer; 113 AA/M Chaplow; 114 AA/M Chaplow; 115 AA/M Chaplow; 116 AA/M Chaplow; 117t AA/M Chaplow; 118t AA/M Chaplow; 118b AA/R Strange; 119 AA/M Chaplow; 120 AA/M Chaplow; 121 AA/M Chaplow; 122t AA/M Chaplow; 123 AA/M Chaplow; 124t AA/M Chaplow; 124bl AA; 124bc AA; 124br AA; 125t AA/M Chaplow; 125bl AA/M Jourdan; 125bc AA; 125r AA/M Jourdan.

Every effort has been made to trace the copyright holders, and we apologise in advance for any accidental errors. We would be happy to apply the corrections in the following edition of this publication.

Titles in the Series